JOB

By

ROY B. ZUCK

❧ ❧ ❧
❧ ❧ ❧

MOODY PRESS

CHICAGO

Library of Congress Cataloging in Publication Data

Zuck, Roy B.
  Job.
  Bibliography: p. 192.
  1. Bible.   O.T.   Job—Commentaries.   I. Title.
  BS1415.3.Z82   223'.1'07   77-27557
  ISBN 0-8024-2017-6

13 14 15 16 Printing/EP/Year 95 94 93 92 91

Printed in the United States of America

Contents

3

Introduction

UNIQUENESS

"Why did this happen to me?"

Over the centuries people have cried that question while agonizing in pain, weeping from grief, languishing over loss.

Emergency major surgery; a protracted terminal illness; a sudden loss of possessions by fire, earthquake, or flood; the premature death of a child; divorce; a recalcitrant teen; a son killed in war; a teen critically injured in a car áccident; a child born with brain damage; a setback in business—these are some of the many adversities and heartaches shared by the human race.

If we could see direct relationships between our sufferings and sins in our lives—connections between our tragedies and our transgressions—we could more readily comprehend the whys of our troubles. But usually problems intrude without explanations. And when we cannot relate our woes directly to some known acts of sin, we conclude that the afflictions are undeserved.

The wail, What did I do to deserve this? reveals a sense of injustice, a feeling that the problems exceed what we rightfully deserve.

Perhaps the most intense example of undeserved suffering is recorded in the book of Job. In a matter of minutes, Job, a wealthy and godly man, lost all his material possessions, all his children, and his health. Then, adding anguish upon anguish, his friends accused him rather than consoled him. Furthermore, God, from all appearances, was intentionally absenting Himself from Job's problems, refusing to hear and rise to his cause.

Yet Job was "blameless, upright, fearing God, and turning away from evil" (1:1). Could any tragedy be *more* unmerited? Should not a godly person be blessed, not badgered, by God?

Throughout the ages, a strange magnetism about the book of

Job has pulled people to its pages. Certainly many individuals have discovered a degree of solace by identifying with Job, whose distresses were agonizingly prolonged; manifestly unfair, as is all suffering for righteousness' sake; and unbelievably intense.

This book's subject—unjust human suffering—makes it an appealing book. Job addresses itself to the global puzzle of suffering, the universal mystery of misery unmerited.

LITERARY STYLE

Two other factors make the book of Job fascinating: its unusual structure and its poetic richness. It has been heralded as a masterpiece unequaled in all literature. "It is as unique in form as it is profound in content."[1]

Martin Luther called it "magnificent and sublime as no other book of Scripture."[2] Bishop Lowth, pioneer scholar on Hebrew poetry, explained that Job stands "single and unparalleled in the Sacred Volume."[3] Thomas Carlyle's often quoted statements about Job merit repeating: "A noble Book; all men's Book! It is our first, oldest statement of the never-ending Problem,—man's destiny, and God's ways with him here in this earth. . . . There is nothing written, I think, in the Bible or out of it, of equal literary merit."[4]

Typical of the assessment made by poets and Bible expositors is the opinion of Victor Hugo, nineteenth-century French essayist, who concluded that Job is perhaps the greatest masterpiece of the human mind. A contemporary writer eulogized the book picturesquely: "Like the Washington Monument, whose foundations are in the soil of the crossroads of human problems and decisions, the Book of Job rises to a majestic monolithic grandeur of its own."[5]

1. Robert Gordis, *Poets, Prophets, and Sages* (Bloomington, Ind.: Indiana U., 1971), p. 281.
2. James Strahan, *The Book of Job Interpreted* (Edinburgh: T. & T. Clark, 1913), p. 28.
3. Robert Lowth, *Lectures on the Sacred Poetry of the Hebrews,* 2 vols. (1787; reprinted, Hildesheim, W. Ger.: Georg Olms Verlag, 1969), 2:347.
4. Thomas Carlyle, "The Hero as a Prophet," *On Heroes, Hero-Worship, and the Heroic in History,* ed. Archibald MacMechan (Boston: Ginn, 1901), pp. 55-56.
5. Wesley C. Baker, *More Than a Man Can Take: A Study of Job,* p. 7.

Why do so many writers praise the book of Job as a literary masterpiece?

1. One reason is its unique structure. It is a mixture of prose and poetry, and of monologue and dialogue. The prologue (1:1—2:13) and the epilogue (42:7-17) are narrative prose, and the lengthy material in between is poetry. Within that poetic section (3:1—42:6) are a monologue by Job, three cycles of dialogues between the friends and Job, and four speeches by a fourth friend. Then God responds to Job and orally displays His splendor in various aspects of nature. Job is silenced and repents of his arrogance before the infinitely wise and powerful God. That concludes the section written in poetry.

The prose-poetry-prose pattern, though seen in other compositions of the ancient Near East,[6] is unique among the books of the Bible.

2. Another reason Job is acclaimed as literature is the richness of its vocabulary. Many Old Testament words are found only in the book of Job. In fact, Job has 110 hapax legomena (words that are not found elsewhere in the Old Testament)—more than any other Old Testament book.[7]

Five different words are used for lions (4:10-11), six for traps (18:8-10), and six for darkness (3:4-6; 10:21-22). As Gordis has observed, the writer "knows the names of the constellations, of metals, and of many precious stones. He is familiar with the detailed anatomy of great beasts, the technical language of the law courts, and the occupations of mining and hunting."[8] References to insects, reptiles, birds, beasts; weapons and military strategies; musical instruments; means of travel; geography; whirlwinds, dew, dawn, darkness, clouds, rain—all reveal the profuse knowledge and the vocabulary of the author of the book of Job.[9] Its rich vocabulary reveals influences from several languages

6. Two examples from Egypt are the "Dispute over Suicide" and the "Protests of the Eloquent Peasant" (James L. Pritchard, ed., *Ancient Near Eastern Texts Relating to the Old Testament* [Princeton: Princeton U., 1955], pp. 405-7).
7. W. B. Stevenson, *The Poem of Job* (London: Geoffrey Cuberlege, 1947), p. 71.
8. Robert Gordis, *The Book of God and Man: A Study of Job*, p. 160.
9. For details, see Albert Barnes, *Notes, Critical, Illustrative, and Practical, on the Book of Job*, 1:lxxi-lxxxii.

besides Hebrew, including Akkadian, Arabic, Aramaic, Sumerian, and Ugaritic.[10]

3. A third literary quality is the book's extensive use of similes and metaphors. As an example, the brevity of life is depicted by a weaver's shuttle (7:6), one's breath (7:7), a cloud (7:9), a shadow (8:9, 14:2), a runner (9:25), a falcon (eagle) (9:26), and a flower (14:2).[11]

Those factors, along with poetic parallelism (two lines per verse, in which the second line completes or contrasts the thought of the first line) and strophes (a strophe is a group of verses in a rhythmic pattern) make the book of Job, as Tennyson has labeled it, "the greatest poem of ancient or modern times."[12]

AUTHOR

The book of Job abounds with mysteries: Who wrote it? When was it written? When did its events occur? Where did Job live? Perhaps those questions, no one of which can be answered with certainty, further add to the charm of the book.

Because the author is not identified, Bible students can only surmise who may have written it. Numerous suggestions have been made, including Job himself, Elihu (the fourth friend, who spoke toward the end of the book [chaps. 32—37]), Moses, Solomon, Hezekiah, Isaiah, someone after the Babylonian Exile such as Ezra, and an anonymous author two hundred years before Christ.

Because of several similarities between Job and Genesis and because of Moses' familiarity with the desert, Jewish tradition says that Job was written by Moses. Other scholars argue for Solomon as the author because of his interest in poetic literature (e.g., Proverbs, Ecclesiastes, Song of Solomon) and a few similarities between Job and Proverbs (e.g., Job 28 and Prov 8).

The details of the lengthy conversations recorded in the book of Job give the impression that it was written by an eyewitness. Certainly Job, who was so intensely involved in the narrative,

---

10. Numerous examples are cited by R. Laird Harris, "The Book of Job and Its Doctrine of God," *Grace Journal* 13 (fall 1976): 10-14.
11. For more examples, see Stevenson, pp. 66-70.
12. Victor E. Reichert, *Job,* p. xiii.

would recall perhaps as well as or better than other eyewitnesses what happened and what was said. In the 140 years he lived after being restored to health, he would have had ample time to compile the work. This view is as plausible as or more plausible than the view that an author hundreds of years later compiled what had been handed down by oral tradition over many centuries.

It was not uncommon in Old Testament times for a person to record events about himself in the third person. Of course, someone else may have written the last two verses, which tell of Job's age and death. That too was not uncommon.

Some scholars suggest that the book was compiled over many years by several authors and editors, each of whom added small portions to the initial work. However, numerous poetic features point to a single author, as several scholars have pointed out.[13] In addition, numerous cross-references within the book point to its unity. Paring away portions of the book to get to an alleged original core destroys the interdependence of all parts of the story.

DATE

The date of the events described in the book of Job must be distinguished from the date of the writing of the book. The latter is related to the question of authorship.

Views on the time when Job lived range all the way from the patriarchal age (Abraham, Isaac, and Jacob—approximately 2100 to 1900 B.C.) to the sixth century B.C. The following factors point to the time of the patriarchs.

1. The length of Job's life corresponds roughly to the length of the patriarchs. All his children were grown, so Job may have been about 60 years old at the time they were killed. After his calamities, he lived another 140 years (42:16).[14] Thus his age of about 200 compares with Terah, Abraham's father, who died at the age of 205; Abraham, who lived to be 175; Isaac, who was 180 when he died; and Jacob, who died at the age of 147.

---

13. E.g., Marvin H. Pope, *Job*, p. xli; and Nahum M. Sarna, "Epic Substratum in the Prose of Job," *Journal of Biblical Literature* 76 (1957):13-25.
14. Some scholars suggest, however, that Job lived 140 years altogether. That would still correspond with the patriarchs' length of life, particularly Jacob's.

Joseph was 110 years old when he died, and the lives of men since that time have been shorter.

2. Job's wealth was reckoned in livestock (1:3; 42:12), which was also true of Abraham (Gen 12:16; 13:2), and Jacob (Gen 30:43; 32:5).

3. The Sabeans and Chaldeans (1:15, 17) were nomads, but they were not nomads in later years.

4. That Job was the priest of his family (1:5) would suggest that an official national priesthood was not yet in existence in Job's area.

5. The Hebrew word translated "piece of money" (42:11) is used elsewhere only twice (Gen 33:19; Josh 24:32), both times in reference to Jacob.

6. The musical instruments referred to (21:12; 30:31), the timbrel, harp (or lyre), and flute (or pipe), are also mentioned in Genesis (4:21; 31:27).

7. Job's daughters were heirs of his estate along with their brothers (42:15). This, however, was not possible later under the Mosaic law (Num 27:8).

8. Literary works similar in some ways to the book of Job were written in Mesopotamia about the same time.

9. The book of Job includes no references to the Mosaic institutions (priesthood, laws, tabernacle, special religious days and events, etc.).

10. The name *Shaddai* is used of God thirty-one times in Job (compared with only seventeen elsewhere in the Old Testament) and is a name familiar to the patriarchs (Gen 17:1, marg.; Exod 6:3, marg.).

11. A number of personal and place names in the book were also associated with the patriarchal period. Examples include Sheba (a grandson of Abraham), and the Sabeans from Sheba (Gen 25:3; Job 1:15; 6:19); Tema (another grandson of Abraham), and Tema (a location in Arabia)[15] (Gen 25:15; Job 6:19); Eliphaz (son of Esau), and Eliphaz (one of Job's com-

---

15. Possibly Eliphaz the Temanite was from Tema in Arabia (or Teman in Edom). Perhaps, too, Bildad the Shuhite was from Shuah, a location named after Abraham's youngest son. And Elihu, the son of Barachel the Buzite, may have been from Buz, the name of Abraham's nephew. Buz is mentioned along with Dedan and Tema, Arabian locations (Jer 25:23).

panions) (Gen 36:4; Job 2:11); Uz (a nephew of Abraham), and Uz (where Job lived) (Gen 22:21; Job 1:1).

Job was a common West Semitic name in the second millennium B.C. The earliest known usage of the name is in a list of kings in Mari (on the upper Euphrates River) dating from 2000 to 1800 B.C. Job is also the name of a nineteenth-century-B.C. prince in the Egyptian Execration texts. Other occurrences of the name are found in the Amarna letters (ca. 1400 B.C.) and in Ugaritic texts.

12. Stylistic parallels to Ugaritic literature lead Sarna to conclude that "the patriarchal setting must be regarded as genuine."[16]

Outline of Job

I. Prologue (in prose) (chaps. 1—2)
   A. Job's character (1:1-5)
     1. His place and piety (1:1)
     2. His prosperity (1:2-3)
     3. His posterity (1:4-5)
   B. Job's calamities (1:6—2:10)
     1. The first test (1:6-22)
     2. The second test (2:1-10)
   C. Job's comforters (2:11-13)

II. Dialogue (in poetry) (3:1—42:6)
   A. Job's complaint (chap. 3)
     1. He wished he had not been born (3:1-10)
     2. He wished he had died at birth (3:11-19)
     3. He wished he could die then (3:20-26)
   B. The first cycle of speeches (chaps. 4—14)
     1. Eliphaz's first speech (chaps. 4—5)
     2. Job's first reply to Eliphaz (chaps. 6—7)
     3. Bildad's first speech (chap. 8)
     4. Job's first reply to Bildad (chaps. 9—10)
     5. Zophar's first speech (chap. 11)
     6. Job's first reply to Zophar (chaps. 12—14)

16. Sarna, p. 25.

C. The second cycle of speeches (chaps. 15—21)
1. Eliphaz's second speech (chap. 15)
2. Job's second reply to Eliphaz (chaps. 16—17)
3. Bildad's second speech (chap. 18)
4. Job's second reply to Bildad (chap. 19)
5. Zophar's second speech (chap. 20)
6. Job's second reply to Zophar (chap. 21)
D. The third cycle of speeches (chaps. 22—31)
1. Eliphaz's third speech (chap. 22)
2. Job's third reply to Eliphaz (chaps. 23—24)
3. Bildad's third speech (chap. 25)
4. Job's third reply to Bildad (chaps. 26—31)
E. Elihu's four speeches (chaps. 32—37)
F. God's confrontation (38:1—42:6)
1. God's first speech (38:1—40:2)
2. Job's first reply to God (40:3-5)
3. God's second speech (40:6—41:34)
4. Job's second reply to God (42:1-6)

III. Epilogue (in prose) (42:7-17)
A. God and Job's friends (42:7-9)
B. God and Job's fortunes (42:10-17)

1

Does Job Serve God for Nothing?

I. PROLOGUE (chaps. 1—2)

In the prose prologue of Job, the issues and characters are set forth swiftly in tense words. Job's spiritual character, his family and possessions, Satan's accusations and attacks on Job, Job's reactions, and the arrival of his friends—all are set before the reader in rapid fashion, as if they were on a film run at fast speed. It all happens so suddenly! By contrast, the following dialogue is like slides projected on the screen for studied review. The pace is slow, the plot is simple. Obviously, the prologue is necessary background told in rapid narrative style in order to get the reader quickly to Job's agonizing confrontation with his friends and God.

A. JOB'S CHARACTER (1:1-5)

First we are introduced to Job's *place* and *piety* (1:1). He lived "in the land of Uz." Like the date and author of Job, the location also is uncertain. The place Uz is mentioned two other times in the Bible: the first says that Uz was a land of kings, at least in Jeremiah's day (Jer 25:20); and the second refers to Uz as a possession or neighbor of Edom (Lam 4:21). Some scholars think that Uz was in the fertile Bashan, south of Damascus; others suggest that Uz was in Edom, southeast of the Dead Sea; and still others point to evidence that places Uz east of Edom, in northern Arabia. The last view is supported by the facts that Job lived near the desert (1:19); his land was fertile for agriculture and livestock-raising (1:3, 14; 42:12); and customs, vocabulary, and references to geography and natural history relate to northern Arabia. Wherever the location, it was outside Palestine and thus

13

"serves ideally as a setting for the universal spirit and character of the message conveyed by the book of Job."[1]

Job was more than a good man. He was (1) "blameless" ("perfect," KJV), which means "without moral blemish," or "morally whole"; (2) "upright," meaning "straight" in the sense of not deviating from God's standards; (3) "fearing God," which means "aware of, revering, and submissive to God's majesty"; and (4) "turning away from evil," meaning "hating and rejecting the opposite of God's character." That assessment, repeated by God to Satan (1:8; 2:3), tells the reader that Job is no ordinary man. It also shows that his friends were totally in error in accusing him of being a willful sinner.

Next the author describes Job's family and his *prosperity* (1:2-3). His sheep provided clothing and food; camels and donkeys provided transportation; and oxen provided food and milk, and the power for plowing (wheat and barley are mentioned [31:38-40]). His possessions also included slaves (1:15-17; 31:13). He was wealthy as well as godly—two characteristics not often found together. He was a remarkable man indeed.

As "the greatest of all the men of the east," he was the wealthiest of an apparently prosperous group of people in northern Arabia. (The "men of the east" are identified with Kedar, which is in the northern portions of Arabia [Jer 49:28].) Job was also unusually wise, for the men of the East were noted for their great wisdom, expressed in proverbs, songs, and stories.

And then the author speaks of Job's *posterity* (1:4-5). His godly character is seen in his concern for the spiritual welfare of his grown children. After each year's round of birthday parties given by each of his seven sons (a "feast" on "his day" [1:4]), Job would offer burnt offerings for forgiveness of any sins committed by them unknowingly or otherwise. In every way, Job was capable and exemplary—in his ability to amass wealth, in his concern for his family, in his godly piety before God. Those sterling qualities make Job's adversities, by contrast, all the more severe. The stark contrast heightens the impact of the

---

1. Charles W. Carter, "The Book of Job," in *The Wesleyan Bible Commentary*, ed. Charles W. Carter, vol. 2 (Grand Rapids: Eerdmans, 1968), p. 14.

book's message to those whose qualifications—and suffering may be less severe than his.

B. Job's Calamities (1:6—2:10)

Job was subjected to two tests—one on his possessions and offspring (1:6-22) and one on his health (2:1-10). In each test are two scenes, one in heaven and one on earth. Each scene in heaven includes an accusation by Satan against Job, and each scene on earth includes an assault by Satan against Job.

On the day the sons of God (angels) presented (literally, "stationed") themselves before God to report on their activities, Satan reported that he was roaming ("going around") and walking on the earth, apparently looking for those whom he could accuse and devour (cf. 1 Pet 5:8). Knowing Satan's searching, the Lord mentioned Job as His supreme example of piety: "there is no one like him on the earth" (1:8), and He called him by the honorable title, "My servant." God was confident that Satan would find in Job more than surface devotion.

Satan's response attacked Job's motives. Because Satan could not deny God's assessment of Job's godliness, he questioned why Job was pious. "It's all a front. He serves You only because of what he gets out of it. Take the pay away and he'll quit the job. Certainly he doesn't serve You for nothing!"

Does Job serve God for nothing? That is a basic question in the book of Job. In addition to causing the reader to ponder why a righteous man should suffer, the book poses the question, through Satan's words, of whether Job's worship has been genuine or self-motivated. *Can one do good for wrong motives.*

Will Job be seen as one who will serve God even if he gets nothing in return? Will *anyone* serve God for no personal gain? Is worship a coin that buys us a heavenly reward? Does man serve God to get blessings, fearing that failure to worship will bring punishment? Is piety part of a contract by which to gain wealth and ward off trouble?

Satan's subtle suggestion that worship is basically selfish hits at the very heart of man's relation to God. "Remove your protecting hedge and Your blessings from his work, and his true colors will show. Subtract what he has and You'll see him for

15

what he truly is—a cursing, self-centered man."[2] That accusation also attacks the integrity of God. As one writer explains it: "Satan is also accusing God of rigging the rules of the game, i.e., He can't get a response from man without a bait."[3] Why God allowed Satan to buffet Job is not fully understood. "Doesn't God already know the motives of his children? Why does he need to test them to find out?"[4] Surely God knows, but He used Job as a demonstration to silence Satan. In addition, He wanted to deepen Job's spiritual insight.

Having gained permission, Satan began his assaults on Job when his ten children were feasting in their eldest brother's house (1:13, 18). The assaults were alternately caused by human and "natural" forces: first, a Sabean attack; second, "the fire of God"; third, a Chaldean raid; fourth, a great desert wind. Satan was able to move both kinds of causes to accomplish his purposes—and to do so according to rapid, precise timing. Job, while reeling in shock from the news of one loss, was stunned with another.

The Sabeans, who stole the 1,000 oxen and 500 donkeys and slaughtered the servants (1:14-15), may have been from the region of Sheba, in southwest Arabia, or from a town called Sheba, near Dedan, in upper Arabia (Gen 10:7; 25:3).

The fire of God, which "fell from heaven and burned up the sheep and the servants" (1:16), may have been caused by lightning. Some surmise that the 7,000 sheep were in a large barn, which caught fire.

The Chaldeans, who attacked in three companies from three sides and stole the 3,000 camels and slaughtered the servants (1:17), were fierce, marauding inhabitants of Mesopotamia. They possibly came from the north, in contrast with the Sabeans, who had come from the south. Apparently the raids by those two groups were surprise attacks.

The great wilderness wind that "struck the four corners of the house" (1:19) suggests a tornado or whirling wind, building in

---

2. In the question "Hast Thou not made a hedge about him?" "Thou" is emphatic.
3. Edgar Jones, *The Triumph of Job* (London: SCM, 1966), p. 29.
4. L. D. Johnson, *Israel's Wisdom: Learn and Live*, p. 56.

momentum as it whipped across the desert. The wind toppled the house, causing it to fall on Job's ten children and kill them.

All Job's livestock had been stolen; all his servants had been murdered (except four messengers who had escaped to report; they were either Job's servants or others who had witnessed the tragedies); and all his children had been killed. In a few minutes, Job had plummeted from wealth and prosperity to grief and pauperism. Would he also plummet from love for God to imprecation of Him?

In the aftermath (1 20-22) of that first assault, Job tore his robe,[5] symbolizing inner turmoil, and shaved his hair, depicting the loss of his personal glory. Falling to the ground, not in despair, but in obeisance to God, Job worshiped God. As his face touched the ground, his body conveyed the attitude of his heart—submission before God in humble worship.

Job recognized that his loss was not unlike his birth and his death: he had been naked at birth, and he would be naked at death. Similarly, now he was naked, not literally, but figuratively: with no possessions and no one to give them to. By "Naked I came from my mother's womb, and naked I shall return there," Job did not mean he longed to go back to the prenatal security of his mother's womb. Instead, he meant the grave, for speaking of the womb of one's mother is a poetic way of referring to the earth (cf. Psalm 139:15; Eccles 5:15; 12:7). The connection is obvious; for man, formed in the womb, is also made "of dust from the ground" (Gen 2:7; 3:19; Job 10:9; 34:15), and the earth, like a mother, gives birth to living things.

Recognizing God's sovereign rights ("the LORD gave and the LORD has taken away" [1:21b]), Job praised the Lord (literally, "Yahweh"). How many believers today would react as Job did if they encountered the blows he experienced? How many would follow adversity with adoration, woe with worship? How many would, like Job, maintain their moral integrity, refusing to bend to bitterness? How many, suffering inequitably, would refuse to blame[6] God of wrongdoing?

Satan lost in his first effort to uncover Job as a worshiper for

5. The robe was worn by men of rank.
6. "Blame" is literally "give or ascribe what is tasteless or inappropriate."

the sake of wealth. Job's amazing response showed Satan to be utterly wrong in predicting that Job would curse God. Devotion *is* possible without the dollar received in return. Man *can* be godly apart from material gain. Job's saintly worship at the moment of extreme loss and intense grief verified God's words.

Satan did not give up, however. In the second test (2:1-10), he again indicted God's word and impugned Job's motives and character. In this third scene, back in heaven, Satan implied that Job was still worshiping God because he had not yet given up his life. "Skin for skin! Yes, all that a man has he will give for his life" (2:4). "Anyone," Satan insinuated, "would give up his possessions and children—all that he has—in order to preserve his own life." "Skin for skin" was a proverbial saying, possibly used to refer to bartering or trading animal skins. "Job has willingly traded the skins [lives] of his own children because in return You have given him his own skin [life]." The statement again implies that Job is selfish. "Sure, he will worship You, so long as You spare his life. But if you touch his body with disease, then, with no further reason for worship, he will curse You."

Receiving permission from God to touch Job's body, but not to take his life, Satan immediately caused Job to have "sore boils from the sole of his foot to the crown of his head" (2:7). Whereas the first test involved Job's wealth, the second one involved his health.

The two Hebrew words translated "sore boils" were used of one of the ten plagues in Egypt (Exod 9:8-11; Deut 28:27) and of Hezekiah's illness (2 Kings 20:7). Some scholars say that the disease may have been smallpox.[7] Others suppose it to be elephantiasis, so-called because of swollen limbs and black, wrinkled skin resembling the hide of an elephant. It was apparently some skin condition with scabs or scales, such as chronic eczema, leprosy, psoriasis, pityriasis, keratosis,[8] or pemphigus foliaceus.[9]

7. A. Rendle Short, *The Bible and Modern Medicine* (Chicago: Moody, 1953), pp. 60-61.
8. C. Raimer Smith, *The Physician Examines the Bible* (New York: Philosophical Library, 1950), p. 60.
9. See Samuel Terrien, "The Book of Job," in *The Interpreter's Bible,* ed. George A. Buttrick, vol. 3 (Nashville: Abingdon, 1954), p. 920; and

The latter seems to fit best the symptoms of Job's afflictions—inflamed, ulcerous sores (2:7), itching (2:8), degenerative changes in facial skin (2:7, 12), loss of appetite (3:24), depression (3:24-25), worms in the boils (7:5), hardened skin and running sores (7:5), difficulty in breathing, figuratively if not literally (9:18), dark eyelids (16:16), foul breath (19:17), loss of weight (19:20; 33:21), continual pain (30:17), restlessness (30:27), blackened skin (30:30), and fever (30:30). It may have lasted for several months at least, because Job referred to his "months of vanity" (7:3) and the "months gone by" (29:2).

The aftermath (2:8-10) of this second assault included three things: Job's separation from the city, his temptation by his wife, and his submission to God.

He sat "among the ashes," that is, on or near the pile of dung ashes and garbage outside the city. Beggars, outcasts, and dogs were present. How indignant and humiliating for one who had sat at the city gate as a local judge (29:7) now to be outside the city walls with beggars, scraping his itching, running sores with a piece of broken pottery!

When his wife urged him to forget his integrity (related to the word "blameless" [1:1]), curse God, and die, he called her a foolish (i.e., spiritually ignorant or nondiscerning) woman (2:10). Her suggestion that he curse God was exactly what Satan had twice said he would do (1:11; 2:5). At the moment when he needed comfort from her, he received another terrible blow—evidence of her bitterness toward God.[10]

His willingness to receive adversity as well as blessing from God shows that he did not serve God for personal gain. The affirmation "In all this Job did not sin with his lips" proved wrong Satan's predictions that Job would curse God, and it vindicated God's words.

Rupert Hallam, "Pemphigus Foliaceus," in *The British Encyclopaedia of Medical Practice*, vol. 9, pp. 490-92.

10. Some expositors view her remark as a word of compassion, as if she were preferring for him a sudden death rather than a prolonged illness. That, however, does not seem to match her recommendation that he withdraw from his moral consistency or wholeness and curse God.

C. JOB'S COMFORTERS (2:11-13)

Having heard about Job's perils, three of his friends—Eliphaz, Bildad, and Zophar, apparently prominent men—visited him. "Eliphaz" is an Edomite name (Gen 36:4), and as a Temanite he was from either Teman in Edom, known for its wisdom (Jer 49:7; Obad 8), or Tema in Arabia. "Bildad" is not used elsewhere in the Bible, and "Shuhite" may suggest a relationship to Shuah, Abraham's youngest son (Gen 25:2). "Zophar" is used only in Job, and his lineage as a Naamathite is unknown, although some have suggested that Naamah, a Judean town (Josh 15:41), was his hometown. A fourth friend, Elihu, was present though he is not mentioned until later (chap. 32).

Eliphaz was probably the eldest of the three, for he is listed first (2:11; 42:9), he spoke first, his speeches are longer and more mature in content, and God addressed him as the representative of the others (42:7).

The three comforters agreed to meet at the same time (apparently arranged by means of personal messengers, for "they came each one from his own place," [2:11]), and their purpose was to sympathize with Job and comfort him.

Because Job was disfigured from the disease, they did not recognize him. Somehow they did know it was Job, for they then expressed their grief and despair in four ways (2:12): they wailed (in emotional shock), wept (in sorrow), tore their robes (in brokenheartedness), and threw dust over their heads to the sky (in deep grief or "in recognition of their helplessness"[11]).

Sitting down in silence with him for a week may have been their way of mourning over his deathlike condition,[12] or it may have been an act of sympathy and comfort. Other explanations for their silence are that the comforters were so horrified at his loss that words of sympathy escaped them, or that they began to reflect in surprise at the possibility of his having been a hypocrite all along, considering his suffering as punishment for sin. Whatever their reasons, they followed the custom of that day and allowed the grieving person to express himself first.

11. Carter, p. 42.
12. The usual time of mourning for the dead was seven days (Gen 50:10; 1 Sam 31:13; Ezek 3:15).

The prologue tells the reader at the start that the friends were wrong in their view that Job's suffering was the result of his sin. The reader is also told something that Job and his comforters themselves did not know—that Satan was the instigator of Job's trouble, and that one of the purposes of his suffering was to answer Satan's question, "Will a man serve God gratis; will he worship if nothing is gained in return?"

2

I Want to Die

II. DIALOGUE (3:1—42:6)

A. JOB'S COMPLAINT (chap. 3)

The silence of Job's friends was broken when Job bemoaned that he had been born and expressed his longing to die. Why did he speak words that are in such shocking contrast to his former expression of calm submission to God? Perhaps the passing of time ingrained his sense of loss and rendered unbearable the relentless pain of his disease. Perhaps, too, time had given him opportunity to reflect on the total injustice of his condition, with death seen as his only escape from such cruelty. Or, his friends' silence may have aggravated him.

In his sad soliloquy of a death wish, Job did not curse God, as Satan had predicted, nor did he contemplate suicide. He "laments his misery, but does not complain of injustice, or lament his integrity."[1]

In this "Niagara of anguish,"[2] Job regretted his birth (3:1-10), wished he had been born dead (3:11-19), and longed to die (3:20-26).

1. *He wished he had not been born* (3:1-10)

Job cursed "the day of his birth" (literally, his day) (3:1), beginning with the words, "Let the day perish on which I was to be born" (3:3). If the day on which he was born had been wiped from the calendar, he could have avoided being born. Job then backed up to the moment at night when he was conceived.

---

1. H. H. Rowley, *Job*, p. 41.
2. Robert N. Schaper, *Why Me God?*, p. 26.

Apparently he considered conception the beginning of his existence. The night was personified as knowing and announcing the sex of the child conceived.[3]

The content of 3:3-10 is arranged in an interesting strophe. First, 3:3 introduces the day of birth, and the night of conception. Then 3:4-5 relate to the day of birth, and 3:6-9 speak of the night of conception. (Note that 3:4 has, in effect, two "let nots"—"Let not God above care for it," and "[Let not] light shine on it"—and that 3:6 has two "let nots.") Then 3:10 concludes the poetic unit with the reason Job longed for the removal of his birthday.

In 3:4, Job pronounced darkness on his birthday as a way of expressing his wish that he had never seen the light of day. "May that day be darkness" is an interesting reversal of God's first-day creative act: "Let there be light" (Gen 1:3). By praying "Let not God above care for it" (literally, seek it or look for it), he was hopeful that God, by not noticing that day, would therefore not notice Job.

The Hebrew language is rich in synonyms, as evidenced in 3:4-6, in which Job refers to darkness five times, using four different words. He longed that the day would be *darkness* (3:4), he asked that *darkness* and *black gloom* would claim it (3:5a), and that *blackness* of the day would terrify it (3:5c). The word "blackness," used only here in the Old Testament, means the blackness that comes from an eclipse, tornado, or heavy storm clouds. In 3:6a, as Job began again to discuss the night, he requested, "Let darkness seize it." The word translated "darkness" means "thick (or deep) darkness," and it is used five times in Job. "Let it not rejoice among the days of the year; let it not come into the number of the months" (3:6b-c) means, "may the night of my conception not be included or counted (literally, rejoice, a poetic personification) in the calendar of days and nights and months." Continuing his personification of the night (3:7), Job prayed that the night would have been barren (lit-

---

3. "Such personifications of day and night are common among the Arabs" (Albert Barnes, *Notes, Critical, Illustrative, and Practical, on the Book of Job,* 1:125).

23

erally, stony), meaning, of course, that his mother would have been barren (as unproductive as stony ground).

Emotional Near Easterners customarily shouted when a boy was born, but Job said, "Let no joyful shout enter [literally, pierce] it [the night]."

Leviathan (3:8) was a seven-headed sea monster of ancient Near Eastern mythology. In the Ugaritic literature of Canaan and Phoenicia, eclipses were said to be caused by Leviathan's swallowing the sun or moon.[4] Job said "Let those curse it [the night of my conception] who curse the day, who are prepared to rouse Leviathan." He was referring to a custom of sorcerers or enchanters, who claimed to have the power to make a day unfortunate by rousing the dragon asleep in the sea and inciting it to swallow the sun or moon. Thus, if the daytime or night-time luminary were gone, Job's birthday would, in a sense, be missing. Was Job indicating belief in a creature of mythology? No, he was probably doing nothing more than utilizing for poetic purposes a common notion that his hearers would understand. This would have been similar to modern adults' referring to Santa Claus. Mentioning his name does not mean that one believes such a person exists.

Seeking to express in every way possible his disdain for his birthday, Job adds, "Let the stars of its twilight [that is, the morning stars after the night of my conception] be darkened; let it wait for light but have none, neither let it see the breaking dawn" (3:9). The morning stars are actually the planets Venus and Mercury, easily seen at dawn because of their brilliance (cf. 38:7). The "breaking dawn" is literally "eyelids of the morning," a metaphor in which the morning rays of sunlight coming over the horizon at dawn are likened to the opening eyelids of a person waking up. The same figure is used later (41:18).

Job did not want light on his conceptual night. And he gave the reason for his imprecations: That night of conception "did not shut the opening of [his] mother's womb, or hide trouble from [his] eyes" (3:10). Opening the womb pictured concep-tion, not birth. Thus, because the womb of his mother did open

4. Leviathan is referred to in five passages: Job 3:8; 41:1; Psalms 74:14; 104:26; Isa 27:1.

24

and he was conceived, Job felt that the night did not "hide trouble from [his] eyes" (3:10b). Normally the darkness of the night would hide objects from one's view, but trouble was not blocked from Job's view.

2. *He wished he had died at birth* (3:11-19)

Because Job's desire for the blotting out of his night of conception and day of birth could not be fulfilled, he longed to have been stillborn. He preferred that to his present condition. After cursing his birthday, he seems to have subsided into a quieter reflection on the trouble-free condition he would enjoy had he been born dead.

Again, in this passage there is an interesting strophic arrangement. The stillbirth, or miscarriage, is mentioned in 3:11-12; the result, namely, rest in death, is in 3:13-15; miscarriage is repeated in 3:16, and the result of rest in death is repeated in 3:17-19.

Job asked two questions at the beginning of this passage: "Why did I not die at birth, come forth from the womb and expire? Why did the knees receive me, and why the breasts, that I should suck?" (3:11-12). In the first question, he wondered why he could not have died as he came out of the womb. Nonexistence would have been better than his present existence of turmoil. In the second question, the receiving of the knees refers either to his mother's taking him in her lap soon after birth, or to the patriarchs' custom of placing a newborn child on the knees of the father as a symbol that the child was received as his own (cf. Gen 48:12). Job also asked why his mother had to give him nourishment from her breasts. Had she not done so, he could have died. The progression in these questions is noteworthy: coming out of the womb, being received on the parent's knees, and being given nourishment as an infant.

Job then stated how much better he would be had he died at birth; death would bring rest, whereas in life he was experiencing trouble (3:13-15). He mentioned four conditions, each one apparently following the other: lain down, been quiet, slept, been at rest (3:13). His condition in death as an infant would have

25

given him an enviable position with exalted personalities: kings, counselors,[5] and rich princes (3:14-15).

Longing to have been a miscarried fetus "which is discarded" (literally, hidden) or buried, and thus to be "as infants that never saw light" (3:16), Job again referred to the restful condition he could have had in Sheol. There the wicked no longer rage (or, "are in turmoil," as the word is later translated [3:26; 14:1]) in their restless sin and rebellion; the weary rest; prisoners are at ease (no longer hearing their taskmaster shouting at them to work harder); the small and the great are together; and the slave is free (3:17-19). Job, weary with agony, would be at rest in death; he would no longer be a captive to his disease; he would be free from his slavery to trouble. This picturesque language expresses the restful condition of the dead in contrast to the restless condition of the living, who suffer. All who suffer intensely like Job can appreciate his longing for release through death.

3. *He wished he could die then* (3:20-26)

For the third time in his soliloquy, Job asked "why?" (3:20). (The other two times are 3:11 and 3:12.) Referring once again to the subject of light and darkness as indicative of life and death, he asked, "Why is light given to him who suffers, and life to the bitter of soul?" (3:20). The Hebrew word for "suffers" is the word from which comes the noun "trouble" (3:10). The theme of the passage (3:20-26) is summarized in 3:21: "Who long for death, but there is none, and dig for it more than for hidden treasures." Neither the quiet waiting nor the anxious effort to die does any good. Death does not come, and like buried treasures it is not found. When sufferers finally do "find the grave," Job said, they "rejoice greatly" (3:22) because death releases them from pain.

The words "Why is light given" (3:23) (the fourth "why" in this chapter) must be supplied to make the meaning clear. The phrase "to a man whose way is hidden, and whom God has hedged in" refers to Job's own condition (whereas he had spo-

---

5. The phrase "who rebuilt ruins for themselves" does not refer to pyramids built by pharaohs, as some expositors have supposed. Instead, it simply means that kings and counselors rebuilt cities that later became ruins, or more likely, rebuilt ruined cities.

ken in the plural about "sufferers" [3:20b-22]). "Job is bewildered because he cannot see his way. He finds himself suddenly hedged in and no path is visible before him."[6] Satan had used the same Hebrew word (here translated as "hedged in") when accusing God of protecting Job (1:10). Now Job used the word to refer to a restricting hedge.[7] His suffering restricted him from having any hope in his future and limited his freedom of movement. Here for the first time Job asserted that God was the cause of his affliction. "My groaning comes at the sight of my food" (3:24) means either that he groaned when he looked at food (because his illness removed his appetite and made food repulsive) or that his groaning was as frequent and regular as his food: that is, it was daily and continuous. Perhaps the latter is to be preferred because of its parallel to the second line of the verse: "my cries pour out like water." The word for "cries" is used of the roaring of a lion (4:10) and may be rendered "groaning" (cf. Psalm 32:3b). His loud groaning under his pain was like the noise and unending nature of a rushing stream of water (3:24b).

"For what I fear comes upon me" (3:25) can be rendered "for what I feared came upon me." At the beginning of Job's trials, as he heard of the loss of one blessing, he feared the loss of another. And hearing of the second one, he feared yet another, and so forth. His restless, turbulent condition is summarized in the conclusion of the soliloquy (3:26): Job could not be quiet and rest because turmoil (literally, agitation; the Hebrew word is also translated "raging" [3:17]) had come.

Job's suffering was physical, intellectual ("why" introduces several of Job's questions [3:11, 12, 20, 23; 7:20, 21; 9:29; 13:24; 21:4; 24:1]), emotional, and spiritual.[8] In his dramatic monologue, Job vented his despair, voiced his bitter complaint, and craved for the grave. Although bitter (3:20), he did not rail. Though accusing God of hedging him in (3:23) and being responsible for his plight, Job did not curse God. Job's cry was a cry of pain and despair, not a cry of defiance. Job voiced

---

6. Rowley, p. 49.
7. Ibid.
8. David Howard, *How Come, God?*, pp. 31-40.

the intensity of his plight but not the injustice of it. That was to come.

Job's yearning for death emphatically underscores the extremities of his pain. Only those godly people who have relished release from life's woes through the gate of death can fully appreciate Job's mournful wail.

3

Conversations at the Garbage Dump

Job's three companions—Eliphaz, Bildad, and Zophar—had
come to him "to sympathize with him and comfort him" (2:11).
No doubt their motives were pure, their intentions honest. Their
week-long silence expressed their sympathy as well as their be-
wilderment and grief. Then when Job broke the silence with his
outcry of anguish, the three felt compelled to speak. Shocked
by his death-desire, they took upon themselves the responsibility
of correcting Job for his brash remarks.

Each friend spoke and was in turn answered by Job. The
cycle occurs three times, with one variation in the third round:
the third friend did not speak a third time.

Several observations about the speeches may be made:

1. Throughout their speeches, the friends remained adamant
in their theological position. Their view was that the righteous
are rewarded and the unrighteous punished, and that Job therefore was a willful sinner in need of repentance. Their syllogistic
reasoning is as follows: (a) All suffering is punishment for sin;
(b) Job is suffering; (c) therefore, Job is a sinner. This cause-
and-effect relationship says that what a man gets depends on what
he has done.[1]

2. The friends became more vitriolic and specific as the
speeches progressed. In the first round (chaps. 4-14), the three
indirectly hinted at Job's sin, urging him to repent if he had
sinned. "But as for me, I would seek God" (Eliphaz [5:8]);
"If you are pure and upright" (Bildad [8:6]); "If iniquity is in
your hand" (Zophar [11:14]).

The second round moved from suggestion to insinuation.
Eliphaz said that the wicked are endangered (chap. 15), Bildad

1. Matitiahu Tsevat, "The Meaning of the Book of Job," *Hebrew Union College Annual* 77 (1966): 75.

stated that they are ensnared and forgotten (chap. 18), and Zophar affirmed that they are shortlived and lose their wealth (chap. 20). They all hoped Job would get the point and know that they were talking about him.

The third round included open accusation. Eliphaz cited six sins of which he said Job was guilty (22:5-9), and Bildad announced outrightly that man is a worm (25:5-6).

3. In every one of his speeches, Job affirmed his innocence. "I have not denied the words of the Holy One" (6:10); "I am guiltless" (9:21); "there is no violence in my hands" (16:17); "I hold fast my righteousness" (27:6).

4. In his first five speeches, Job stated that God had afflicted him. "The arrows of the Almighty are within me" (6:4); "He bruises me with a tempest" (9:17); "Thou dost put my feet in the stocks (13:27); "He shattered me; . . . He has also set me up as His target" (16:12); "He has . . . considered me as His enemy" (19:11). Job felt that God was cruel to man and would not leave him alone.

5. In each of his three speeches in the first round, Job asked "why?" "Why has Thou set me as Thy target?" (7:20); "Let me know why Thou dost contend with me" (10:2); "Why dost Thou hide Thy face?" (13:24).

6. In six of Job's eight speeches, he longed to present his case to God. "If one wished to dispute with Him, He could not answer Him" (9:3); "I desire to argue with God" (13:3); "O that a man might plead with God" (16:21). "Oh that my words were . . . inscribed in a book" (19:23); "I would present my case before Him" (23:4); "Behold, here is my signature; Let the Almighty answer me!" (31:35).

7. Each of Job's speeches is longer than the one by the friend who spoke immediately before him. Also, each time one of the friends spoke, his speech was shorter than his own preceding speech, except for Zophar, who spoke only twice (chaps. 11, 20).

8. The companions stressed different aspects of God. Eliphaz pointed up the distance between God and man (4:17-19; 15:14-16) and said that God punishes the wicked (5:12-14). Bil-

dad stated that God is just (8:3) and great (25:2-3), and that he punishes only the wicked (18:5-21). Zophar underlined the fact that God is inscrutable (11:7) and that He punishes the wicked quickly (20:23).

9. Eliphaz based his arguments on experience. Three times he said, "I have seen" (4:8; 5:3; 15:17). Bildad was more severe and less courteous than Eliphaz and based his approach on tradition: "inquire of past generations" (8:8). Zophar was the most harsh and blunt of the three. With a sharp tongue and in discourteous dogmatism he pounced on Job. His words were based on mere assumption. "They all condemn Job; for on their philosophy, they must either justify Job at God's expense or justify God at Job's; and, understandably, they chose the latter."[2]

10. Bildad and Zophar, although speaking with emphases different from Eliphaz's, echoed his speeches. They repeated many of the topics Eliphaz had opened. He had said that God is great (5:9; 22:12) and they repeated it (Bildad [8:3, 5, where he calls God "the Almighty"; 25:2a]; Zophar [11:7, 11]). Eliphaz had said that the wicked will be barren (15:32-34), and Bildad (18:16) and Zophar made similar remarks (20:21-22). Eliphaz said that the sinful meet with darkness (5:14), and Bildad (18:5, 6, 18) and Zophar (20:26) reiterated the same observation.

B. THE FIRST CYCLE OF SPEECHES (chaps. 4—14)

1. *Eliphaz's first speech* (chaps. 4—5)

Eliphaz's first address to Job is in five parts: (*a*) his rebuke of Job (4:1-6), (*b*) his reasoning about suffering (4:7-11), (*c*) his report of a vision (4:12-21), (*d*) his recommendation to Job (5:1-17), and (*e*) his reminder of God's blessings (5:18-27).

a. *His rebuke of Job* (4:1-6). As Eliphaz, no doubt the oldest of the three, began his discourse on the ash-heap, he spoke courteously but soon became harsh and cutting. Aware that Job's solo tirade had been an impatient outburst against his troubles, Eliphaz feared that any words he could speak might be met by

2. J. Sidlow Baxter, *Explore the Book,* 6 vols. (London: Marshall, Morgan & Scott, 1952), 3:51.

Job with a similar or stronger impetuosity. "If one ventures a word with you, will you become impatient?" (4:2a).[3]

Eliphaz commended Job for having "admonished many," for having strengthened "weak hands" and "feeble knees," and for having kept the "tottering" on their feet emotionally and spiritually by his words (i.e., counsel) (4:3-4). But that compliment had in it a rebuke, for Job was now unable to take his own medicine. He had advised others to be patient under trial, but now trouble "has come to you, and you are impatient; it touches you, and you are dismayed" (literally, you are in panic). Job had been a great encourager, but he could not encourage himself. What Eliphaz failed to realize is that one who is suffering cannot easily encourage himself; Eliphaz should have been the one to encourage Job!

"Is not your fear of God your confidence, and the integrity of your ways your hope?" (4:6) is either a rebuke of Job for his lack of confidence because he was no longer fearing God, or it is a reminder that because Job had had reverence for God in the past he could also trust Him now.

b. *His reasoning about suffering* (4:7-11). In these verses Eliphaz made a classic statement on his theory of suffering: the innocent do not perish, the upright are not destroyed; but the person who plows iniquity and sows trouble will also harvest trouble[4] (cf. Prov 22:8; Hos 8:7; 10:13), and the wicked perish under God's anger. "The good guys always win, and the bad guys always lose" is a theme all three companions repeat in one way or another throughout the book. "The roaring of the lion and the voice of the fierce lion, and the teeth of the young lions are broken" (4:10) alludes to Job's cry that his former strength had been shattered (chap. 3). As "the lion [literally, lioness] perishes for lack of prey," so Job was helpless; and as "the whelps [lion cubs] of the lioness[5] are scattered" (4:11) by a hunter attacking a lion's den, so Job lost his children.

---

3. This may more accurately be rendered, "Should one venture a word with you while you are so upset!" (cf. Francis I. Andersen, *Job: An Introduction and Commentary,* p. 110, fn. 2).
4. This is the same Hebrew word ("trouble") that Job had used earlier (3:10; and 3:20, where it is translated as "suffers").
5. In these two verses, five different words are used for lion.

c. *His report of a vision* (4:12-21). Eliphaz sought to add authority to his theological viewpoint by relating his experience as if it had occurred in a dream. In his fright, his bones had shaken (4:14) and his hair had stood on end (4:15). The indistinct form of the spirit (4:16) must have been unusually disturbing as he saw it pass by, then stop, remain quiet, and speak in a whisper (4:12, 15-16). Apparently the words that Eliphaz claimed he had heard in his dream are given in verses 17-21. It is questionable whether the words were a revelation from God, because "a word," not "a word of the Lord," came to Eliphaz; because the word came "stealthily" (i.e., in an elusive manner) (4:12); and because the message seems to picture God as unconcerned about man.

"Can mankind [literally, weak, mortal man] be just before God?[6] Can a man [literally, a strong man] be pure before his Maker?" As 4:18-21 indicate, Eliphaz implied a negative answer: Man cannot be righteous and clean before God. God does not trust His servants (angels) and He charges angels (i.e., fallen angels and Satan) with error,[7] so man certainly cannot be trusted. Man's mortality is pictured in several ways: He lives in mere perishable houses made of clay and built on dust, he is easily crushed like a moth, he is broken in pieces like a vessel (cf. Eccles 12:6), and his tent-cord is plucked up (4:19-21). Eliphaz said that man perishes, dying unnoticed (4:20) and without wisdom (4:21). To die without ever finding wisdom was the ultimate disaster for a wise man of the East.

Are the words from Eliphaz's dream true? Yes, in one sense. Man by himself cannot be righteous and pure before God; God charges man with sin more so than the angels; and man is mortal, easily perishing. However, Eliphaz seems to be wrong in applying those words to Job as if he were a willful sinner. To say "The reason you are perishing, Job, is that you are mortal and unclean; there is no hope for you" runs counter to God's evaluation of Job's character (1:1, 8; 2:3). The dream-report seems to be nothing more than another way for Eliphaz to say, "those who

6. Not "can man be *more* just than God?" as some versions erroneously translate the Hebrew.
7. Not "folly" as some translations render the Hebrew.

plow iniquity . . . harvest it" (4:8)—an indirect suggestion that Job is getting what he deserves. Some comfort that would be!

d. *His recomendation to Job* (5:1-17). Eliphaz denied any possibility of angels' ("holy ones' ") intervention on Job's behalf (5:1), because the angels cannot be trusted (4:18). This taunt by Eliphaz seemed to anticipate Job's later regret regarding the absence of a mediator (9:33). Eliphaz interpreted Job's lament (chap. 3) as the "vexation" of a "foolish man" (5:2) and as a simpleton's outburst of "anger," which would kill, not heal.

Eliphaz then stated that he had no regard for a fool; he had even cursed a prospering fool (5:3)! Eliphaz mercilessly reminded Job of his calamities by speaking of the loss of his children and the marauding of his wealth (5:4-5). According to Eliphaz, the source of those afflictions is not the dust or the ground (i.e., mere accident): rather, they come from within man (5:6). Man is born for trouble as certainly as flames from an open fire fly upward (5:7).[8] Eliphaz's view that man by his sin brings trouble on himself, though a partial truth, overlooks Jesus' statement that a falling tower may kill people who were no more sinful than the survivors (Luke 13:4).

In light of his cause-and-effect view of sin, Eliphaz offered his advice: "As for me, I would seek God, and I would place my cause before God" (5:8). That approach—"if I were in your place"—was of little help, for Eliphaz was not and had never been in Job's place. The reason Job should appeal to God, Eliphaz suggested, is that He is majestic, powerful (5:9), and benevolent, sending rain on crops (5:10); He encourages and helps the downcast (5:11), frustrates the shrewd (5:12-14), and delivers the poor and the helpless (5:15-16).[9] Although that advice was not wrong in itself, Eliphaz was wrong in basing his advice on the assumption that Job had sinned deliberately. Even so, Job did seek to present his cause to God.

Another generalization misapplied to Job is in 5:17: "Behold,

8. Some translators wrongly render the verse "man begets trouble." The words "sparks" is literally "sons of Resheph," perhaps a poetic allusion to the Ugaritic god of lightning, pestilence, and flames.

9. "The sword of their mouth" (5:15) picturesquely refers to slander. When God delivers, "unrighteousness must shut its mouth" (5:16); that is, injustice brought about by slander ceases.

how happy is the man whom God reproves, so do not despise the discipline of the Almighty." Eliphaz wrongly assumed that Job's afflictions were disciplinary in nature. His advice to Job, then, was to endure the discipline and not despise it.

e. *His reminder of God's blessings* (5:18-27). If Job would acknowledge his guilt, God would bless. He would give relief; healing; deliverance from famine, war, slander ("the scourge of the tongue" [5:21]), violence, wild beasts (5:18-22);[10] good crops;[11] security; numerous descendants; health; and a long life (5:18-26). Coming to the grave in full vigor "like the stacking of grain in its season" beautifully pictures a life lived to the full and ready to be ended (cf. 42:17).

Eliphaz smugly concluded his first speech by reminding Job of the authority of his observations ("we have investigated it") and by urging him to listen to it and know what Eliphaz has said (5:27). He seemed to have said, "I have the truth, so you might as well face up to it and act accordingly."

In summary, Eliphaz has said that (*a*) Job's suffering is the result of his sin, (*b*) man has no chance before God of being pure, (*c*) man is mortal, (*d*) trouble is not accidental, but retributive or disciplinary, (*e*) God is transcendent, (*f*) submitting to God's ways will bring blessings. Points *c, e,* and *f* are true, but Eliphaz was wrong in his underlying assumption that Job had deliberately turned from God.

2. *Job's first reply to Eliphaz* (chaps. 6—7)

The first reply of Job may be divided as follows: (*a*) his defense of his complaining (6:1-7), (*b*) his despair in his suffering (6:8-13), (*c*) his disappointment in his friends (6:14-23), (*d*) his plea to the three counselors (6:24-30), (*e*) his pattern of misery (7:1-6), and (*f*) his prayer to God (7:7-21).

Rather than begin with a direct response to Eliphaz, Job be-

10. "From six troubles He will deliver you, even in seven evil will not touch you" (5:19) is typical of Old Testament passages that cite one number and then follow it with the next highest number to express completion or thoroughness (cf. Prov 30:15, 18, 21, 29; Amos 1:3, 6, 9, 11, 13; 2:1, 4, 6). If that is the case here, Elihu was saying that God would deliver Job from all kinds of troubles, some of which are then mentioned (5:20-22).

11. "You will be in league with the stones of the field" (5:23) means "the stones will not hinder you from sowing crops."

gan with another complaint about his condition. Then when he did reply to Eliphaz's speech, he addressed all three men, not just Eliphaz. ("Your" and "you" [6:24-30] are plural.) In 7:12-21 he addressed God directly for the first time in the discourses.

a. *Job's defense of his complaining* (6:1-7). Chapter 6 is a chapter of alienation. Job felt that he was alienated from God (6:1-7), from himself (6:8-13), and from his friends (6:14-23).[12] In these first seven verses, the patriarchal sufferer expressed his reason for complaining. "Why shouldn't I complain?" he asked. His "vexation" (or irritation) had been heavy. If it were weighed on one pan of a balance, with his calamities on the other pan, it would be evident that his grief had been heavier (6:2-3).[13] Even the sand of the seas would not be as weighty as his afflictions. What a picturesque way to express his burdens, for wet sand is unusually heavy.

"Therefore my words have been rash" (6:3). Job justified his seemingly reckless previous words (chap. 3) by suggesting this his words were nothing compared to his suffering.

Job felt that God was attacking him directly—shooting poisoned arrows that spread snake venom through his body. Like Eliphaz, Job believed that his distresses came from God. Eliphaz, however, said they were caused by Job's sin, whereas Job denied that connection. To him, the problems were more difficult to bear simply because he believed that they were from God. "The God he had known and the God he now experiences seemed irreconcilable."[14] Does that not give Job cause for complaint? Surely it does, Job suggested. As a wild donkey does not bray or an ox does not low when it has food, so Job would not have complained if his situation were comfortable (6:5).

Tasteless food requires salt; the two go together. So Job's trouble and his wailing go together (6:6), and his complaining should be excused. Verse 7, though interpreted variously, may simply mean that Job refused to touch bland food (cf. 3:24).

12. Kenneth Thompson, Jr., "Out of the Whirlwind: The Sense of Alienation in the Book of Job," *Interpretation* 14 (1960): 51-63.
13. The word "iniquity" (6:2), which occurs only here in the Old Testament, should be rendered "calamity" or "misfortune." It may be related to the subsequent word rendered "calamities" (6:30).
14. H. H. Rowley, *Job*, p. 67.

Implied in that interpretation is the thought that just as he deplored bland food, so he protested his present condition.

b. *Job's despair in his suffering* (6:8-13). Although Job knew that God was the source of his trouble, he also knew that God was the sustainer of life. Therefore, he voiced his "request" and "longing" that God would crush him, loose His hand from sustaining his life, and cut him off (6:8-9). The Hebrew verb translated "loose" carries the idea of setting prisoners free (e.g., Psalm 105:20) and the Hebrew verb rendered "cut off" pictures a weaver cutting thread. If God would let him die, freeing him from life, Job would have one point of consolation, namely, that he did not deny God's words. In fact, he could even endure deep pain, if he knew he could die soon (6:10).

But how can he keep going? "What is my strength, that I should wait? And what is my end, that I should endure?" (6: 11).[15] What was there to hope for? Why should he have undergone such pain? Did Eliphaz think that Job had the strength of stones or that he was as insensitive as bronze (6:12)? The next question (6:13) should be taken as a statement, for the verse is introduced by a strong affirmative particle meaning "indeed." Thus Job stated that he had no help in himself and no resources. Certainly Job was desperate—no hope *for* which to live, and no help or strength *by* which to live.

3. *Job's disappointment in his friends* (6:14-23). When a man is in despair, his friend ought to show him kindness (literally, loyalty) (6:14*a*). Job suggested by his words that Eliphaz had disappointed him by not being loyal. Instead of lashing out at Job, Eliphaz should have been loyal to him. "Lest he forsake the fear of the Almighty" (6:14*b*), is understood by some scholars to describe Eliphaz (by being disloyal he is forsaking the fear of the Almighty). Perhaps a better way is to understand the phrase as referring to Job: without the support of his friends, Job may turn (or is turning) from God.

His friends had been like a riverbed. In the rainy season, a wadi is filled with rushing, raging water ("torrents"), but in the summer it vanishes or dries up just when it is most needed. So

---

15. The word "endure" is literally "prolong my soul," i.e., "be patient." One who is impatient is "short of soul."

his friends, Job asserts, have "acted deceitfully," pretending to help but offering no help at all (6:15). They have become like a mirage.

The riverbeds are turbid (i.e., darkened or filled) with the melting ice and are covered with melting snow (6:16), but then they are silent (i.e., they stop flowing) and vanish in the heat (6:17). Travelers expect to find water in them, but are disappointed. The riverbeds "deceive" them.

"Paths" (6:18) should be rendered "caravans" (the same word used earlier [6:19]), and the verse should read, "Caravans follow their winding course [i.e., the desolate desert] and perish."

Caravans from Tema, in northern Arabia, and Sheba,[16] in southwestern Arabia, both known for their trading, have been lost looking for water in the riverbeds (6:19).

Merchants in camel caravans not only become lost following dry wadis, but they are disappointed and confused when even an oasis is dry (6:20). "You have now become such," Job said pointedly to the three counselors. "You see a terror and are afraid" (6:21). Why should their seeing Job's appearance ("a terror") have caused them fear? Rowley gives this explanation: "Job charges them with cowardice in withholding their sympathy from him, afraid lest they should become sharers of the calamity if they provoked God by showing sympathy with one whom they judged to have offended God."[17] Perhaps they feared guilt by association.[18]

If Job had asked them for something—a bribe (to influence a judge) or deliverance (to free him from overpowering enemies)—he could understand their fear of getting involved. But he had done nothing of the kind (6:22-23).

d. *Job's plea to the three counselors* (6:24-30). Having voiced his keen disappointment in his friends' lack of friendship, Job then pleaded with them to tell him where he had gone wrong. "Where's the evidence for your suggestion that I have sinned?"

---

16. The Sabeans (from Sheba), who were previously referred to (1:15), were raiders; here they are merchants.
17. Rowley, pp. 73-74.
18. Andrew W. Blackwood, Jr., *Devotional Introduction to Job* (Grand Rapids: Baker, 1959), p. 65.

Bible scholars differ on how to render the first line of 6:25. Some suggest, "How painful are honest words"; others say, "How strong [i.e., forceful] are honest words"; still others prefer, "How sweet are honest words." Because the word usually means "grievous" or "painful" (the verbal form is later rendered "plagues" [Job 16:3b], Job's point is possibly this: "I could benefit from honest words even though they might be painful, but how do *your* words help?"

Job then asked how they could reprove him with their words when they considered his words to "belong to the wind" (6:26). How were their words any better than his? The three friends were as unconcerned for him as if they were selling him as a slave, dickering over the price, seeking to gain from his loss (6:27).

Job challenged them again to note his sincerity ("see if I lie" [6:28]), to change their approach ("desist" means "turn," or "change one's mind" [6:29]), and not to be unfair, while recognizing that his justice was involved. They should not be "unjust," for he certainly was not. His palate could still "discern calamities"; that is, he could understand the "flavor" of his sufferings and know if they were deserved (6:30).

e. *Job's pattern of misery* (7:1-6). Because he could taste the flavor of his misfortunes (6:30), Job expressed another bitter complaint of his miserable condition. (The complaint is reminiscent of chapter 3.) Job says that man is like a hired hand, destined to hard labor (7:1), like a slave who works in the hot sun and longs for the shade at the end of the day (7:2a), and like a hired hand waiting to be paid (7:2b). Man's existence is servitude, in which he is subject to continual toil and misery, and in which he hopes for some slight respite.

Although Job's experience was similar to that of the slave and hired workers, his condition was worse. He had months, not just days, of emptiness and worthlessness; and instead of being able to rest in the shade at the end of the day, his nights were filled with trouble (7:3). (The word "trouble," or "toil," is the word already seen earlier [3:10; 4:8; 5:6-7].) His miserable nights are described as anguish ("I am continually tossing" is literally, "I am full of tossing") (7:4). Job's experience obviously was worse than the life of a slave or hired laborer, who could at least rest at night.

Having described his nights as long, he spoke of his days as passing swiftly, moving rapidly like a weaver's shuttle and ending without any hope of his being restored to his former state of blessing (7:6).[19] Between 7:4 and 7:6, however, he described in 7:5 his deplorable physical condition, perhaps as an explanation of his nightly tossing. His flesh was covered with worms, which had got into his open sores, and with dirty scabs (literally, clods of dust). His skin hardened (or cracked) and ran; that is, the scabs cracked and opened, allowing pus or other infected fluids to ooze out.

f. *Job's prayer to God* (7:7-21). Although Job despaired of life, he did not pray for death, as he had in chapter 3—perhaps a hint that his faith was rising as he then turned to God in prayer.[20]

Job first spoke of the brevity and finality of life: his life was as short as a breath[21] (7:7; also stated later [7:16]) and like a vanishing cloud (7:9). When he would die, he would no longer enjoy the good things of this life (perhaps this is an answer to Eliphaz, who had said that Job could be blessed again [5:19-26]), God would behold him no more, and he would never return to his house (7:7-10). He would go down to Sheol, the place of the departed dead, and never return. Thus, when death comes, life as we know it on the earth will never again be the same. Death to Job would be a release from the haunting eyes of God (the third of three occurrences of "eye" and "eyes" in 7:7-8).

After asking God to remember the brevity of his life, Job spoke without restraint in bitter complaint to God (7:11). "Am I the sea or the sea monster, that Thou dost set a guard over me?" (7:12). Job complained that he was being harassed by God. Job

---

19. Interestingly, the words for "hope" and "thread" are the same, thus making an intriguing play on words. As the shuttle runs out of thread, so Job had run out of hope.

20. Charles W. Carter, "The Book of Job," in *The Wesleyan Bible Commentary*, ed. Charles W. Carter, vol. 2 (Grand Rapids: Eerdmans, 1968), p. 65.

21. Physical life, of course, is actually a process of one breath after another, implanted in the first man directly by God (Gen 2:7).

felt that he was like the sea or a sea monster—constantly watched and restrained by God. This is an allusion either to Ugaritic mythology in which the sea god Yam was defeated by Baal or to the Babylonian myth in which Marduk overcame the sea monster Tiamat and set a guard over her.[22] Of course, Job was not giving credence to those myths, but he was using known stories to depict his condition. Like the sea or sea monster dominated and confined by a false god, so Job felt as if were in a subhuman condition in which the true God was guarding him like a defeated enemy. Although Job was speaking unrestrainedly, he was restrained by God.

Job then accused God of frightening him with dreams so that he could not even escape from his problems by sleep (7:13-14). Job again expressed his desire to end his misery by death: "my soul would choose suffocation [or strangling], death rather than my pains" (7:15). The second line may be read, "my bones would choose death."[23]

Because he would not live, Job longed for God to leave him alone (7:16). Verses 17 and 18 are similar to Psalm 8:4, except that the words in the psalm express awe at God's concern, whereas Job expressed remorse that he was haunted continually by God—examined every morning and tested every minute. In frustration, Job felt that God gazed at him continually and would not even leave him alone long enough to swallow his saliva (7: 19)!

Earlier, Job had asked his friends for evidence that he had sinned (6:24). Now he asked God for the same: "Have I sinned?[24] What have I done to Thee, O watcher of men?" (7: 20). Job could not understand why God should be punishing him for some sin he had done to God. He could not understand why God had set him up as a target, an object to strike at, treating him as something bothersome: "Why hast Thou set me as Thy target, so that I am a burden to myself?" (7:20).[25]

"If I am a sinner," Job pleaded, "Why doesn't God forgive

22. See James L. Pritchard, ed., *Ancient Near Eastern Texts Relating to the Old Testament* (Princeton: Princeton U., 1955), p. 67.
23. See Marvin H. Pope, *Job*, p. 62.
24. This is Job's first use of the word "sin."
25. "Myself" may be read "Thee."

41

me my sins [he used three words for sin in 7:20-21: "sin," "transgression," "iniquity"] and be done with it? Why the fuss about a little sin—if I've sinned at all?"

"Then Job tries to get the last laugh on God. . . . 'You'll be sorry when I'm six feet under.' "[26] Having said that God should not be so concerned about and disturbed by man (guarding him like an enemy sea monster, terrifying him with nightmares, caring for and examining and testing Him regularly, gazing on him continually in perpetual surveillance as the "watcher of men," and striking at him), Job now stated that the time would come when God could no longer toy with and tantalize His puny enemy, Job: "I will lie down in the dust; and Thou wilt seek me, but I will not be" (7:21; cf. 7:8). Job would soon be dead; so if God wanted to grant him forgiveness, He should do so at once. In those last words, Job sarcastically combined both a sense of victory and a sense of defeat—victory, in that he would finally get out from under God's constant molesting; and defeat, in that he would be dead.

Thus this prayer to God is a cry of bitter despair: Job was constantly harassed by God, but he would soon be gone. There is bitterness in both life and death.

26. Robert N. Schaper, *Why Me, God?*, p. 44.

4

Do the Bad Guys Always Lose?

3. *Bildad's first speech* (chap. 8)

Like Eliphaz, Bildad held the common view that man's calamities are the consequence of his iniquities. Also like Eliphaz, Bildad pointed Job to the possibility of recovery if he would acknowledge his wrongdoing.

However, whereas Eliphaz had based his arguments on his observation ("I have seen" [4:8]) and his experience (the terrifying dream with its whispered words from a spirit [4:12-21]), Bildad appealed to antiquity, the experience of others. Possibly younger than Eliphaz, Bildad attempted to outdo him by appealing to an even greater authority than Eliphaz's. "Past generations" and "their fathers" (8:8) would surely carry weight with Job, causing him to see the deep error of his rash claim to innocence.

a. *The statement of God's justice* (8:1-7). Whereas Eliphaz had begun politely, Bildad in his shorter speech began abruptly. Eliphaz began with a question that was soft and courteous, but Bildad's opening query was blunt and discourteous. When Bildad asked, "How long will you say these things, and the words of your mouth be a mighty wind?" (8:2), he was expressing his anger with Job for not accepting Eliphaz's gentle rebuke. Job's words (chaps. 6 and 7)—in which he sought to justify his complaining, voiced keen disappointment with his friends, and accused God of unjustly hunting and haunting him—were nothing but a "big[1] wind," blowing wildly, noisily, rashly, and purposelessly, with damaging results. Bildad may have been picking up Job's own reference to wind (6:26).

1. The unusual Hebrew word for "big" or "mighty" suggests that the wind was both strong and abundant; i.e., Job's words were like a lengthy and heavy windstorm (E. Dhorme, *A Commentary on the Book of Job*, p. 112).

In a second question, Bildad then accused Job of perverting (distorting) God's justice and righteousness (8:3). The repetition of "pervert" in both lines of this verse stresses the enormity of Job's coarse words against God. If Job had *not* sinned, his suffering would be evidence of God's perversion of His standards of moral order in the universe. Because God cannot be perverse, the conclusion is clear: Job sinned.

With thoughtless cruelty, Bildad referred to Job's dead children in an effort to demonstrate his point. God "delivered them into the power of their transgression" (8:4) because they sinned against God. Bildad thus hinted that Job's sacrifices for his children (1:5) had no expiatory value; they died because they sinned. And that was why Job was dying.

God would "rouse Himself" on Job's behalf and restore his "righteous estate" to a level of wealth greater than his former position *if* Job would seek God, implore the compassion (literally, grace) of the Almighty Shaddai, also used earlier [8:3, see marg.] and be pure and upright (8:5-6). Eliphaz had made a similar suggestion : "I would seek God" (5:8), with a promise of similar results (5:17-26).

Perhaps Bildad was saying, "There is hope for you if you get right before God." Or he may have been saying, "Because God is not doing anything on your behalf, it is obvious that you are not pure or upright." If the latter meaning is intended, it relates well to Eliphaz's words, "Can a man be pure before his Maker?" (4:17).

b. *The proof of history* (8:8-10). Bildad urged Job to look into history. He would find on investigation that the truths found by their forefathers of many previous generations would confirm Bildad's view (8:8). He gave two reasons for this suggestion (8:9-10): Each individual's life is brief ("of yesterday" and "as a shadow"), with the result that his own knowledge is extremely limited (we "know nothing"), and the ancients possess great wisdom (they can teach us with "words from their minds"). By those last words, Bildad was sarcastically hinting that Job's words were from his mouth only and not from his mind (cf. "the words of your mouth" [8:2]). According to Bildad, Job's idea that he was suffering without having willfully sinned was contrary to the past and therefore wrong. "Bildad's position is that what is true is not new, and what is new is not true."[2]

c. *The paths of the ungodly* (8:11-19). Bildad then used two illustrations from plant life to depict the precarious position of the ungodly. Just as a papyrus plant and reeds cannot grow without water and so wither without even being cut, the wicked cannot sustain themselves without uprightness, and they soon lose their evident prosperity (8:11-13). Job's problems stem from his having forgotten God and his lack of hope stems from his being godless[3]—the exact opposite of God's assessment of Job (1:1, 8).

What the godless man relies on to protect him from ruin will prove as flimsy and useless as a spider's web (8:14).[4] He will lean on and hold to his house (meaning, in the broad sense, his family, establishment, and resources[5]), but it will not give him any support. Bildad insinuated that Job was depending on his possessions for his security—another heartless perversion of the facts.

The second illustration Bildad used from botany is in 8:16-19. A green plant may thrive (or be lush or moist) though in the sun, its branches filling the garden and its roots spreading among the stones; but if it is uprooted, the place where it was growing disowns it. It will no longer flourish ("this is the joy of [its] way" [8:19]), and others will spring up from the soil where that one grew. Similarly, according to Bildad, godless Job, though prospering in vast wealth, was uprooted from his prosperity and others would come along in his place.

d. *The possibility of blessing* (8:20-22). Applying the two botanical illustrations to Job, Bildad asserted his position that God will neither reject a man of integrity (the same word is earlier translated as "blameless" [1:1, 8; 2:3]) nor, on the other hand, support evildoers. Implied in the promises of 8:21-22 is

---

2. S. R. Driver and G. B. Gray, *A Critical and Exegetical Commentary on the Book of Job,* p. 78.
3. The word "godless," used eight times in Job, means "profane" or "irreligious."
4. "Web" is literally "house."
5. Driver and Gray, p. 78.

the condition stated in 8:6: "if you are pure and upright." If Job were to follow Bildad's advice, recognizing his sin and seeking God, he would again enjoy laughter. On the other hand, Bildad concluded (8:20b, 22b) that if Job were an evildoer, God would not support him no matter what he said, and his tent would be gone (i.e., he would have no security or protection, for a man whose tent has been blown away is subject to violent storms and the beating sun).

Bildad's speech missed the mark; it failed to bring comfort and it failed to evince confession of sin. His backward look to history was of no help to Job, for Job's experience was the opposite of the forefathers' wisdom; Bildad's use of illustrations from the present were in conflict with Job's righteous state; and Bildad's prospect of relief in the future failed to console Job in the present. "Life's tragic inequities grinned at all the glib talk about a just God."[6]

4. Job's first reply to Bildad (chaps. 9—10)

a. *God's greatness* (9:1-12). Ignoring some of Bildad's cutting remarks, Job responded, "In truth I know that this is so" (9:2). Perhaps he was acknowledging the validity of Bildad's words that all who forgot God are cut off. But Job reasoned, I have not forsaken God, so why should I be perishing? This raised in his mind the question, "How can a man be in the right before God?" (9:2b). In raising this question, he turned from answering Bildad to interact with Eliphaz's remarks, for that question is almost word for word what Eliphaz had reported from his dream, "Can mankind [the Hebrew means weak or mortal man] be just before God?" (4:17). If Job were to follow Eliphaz's urging that he "place [his] cause before God" (5:8), the problem to be faced would be "how?" Because God had tormented Job, an *upright* man, how, he reasoned, could *any* man stand righteous before God? What hope could there be before such an almighty, arbitrary God?[7]

6. Paul Scherer, "The Book of Job: Exposition," *The Interpreter's Bible,* ed. George A. Buttrick, 12 vols. (Nashville: Abingdon, 1954), 3:974.
7. Implied is a rejection of the accepted orthodoxy of his visitors: "If I apply your theory, *no* man has a chance before God."

Job then proceeded to answer his own question by stating that man cannot dispute (debate in a court case) with God and expect to win (9:3). (When God later appeared to Job, Job found that to be true [see 40:1-5; 42:2].) Job delineated several reasons why it seemed useless to present his case to God:

1. If I disputed with Him, I could not answer Him, because He is so mighty (9:3-14).

2. If God did respond to my cry, I do not think He would be listening, because He is against me (9:15-19).

3. If I am righteous, He will declare me guilty, because He destroys both the innocent and the wicked (9:20-24).

4. If I try to forget my problems or even confess my sins, He would still consider me guilty (9:25-32).

Job was thus ironically conceding the truth of his friends' words about God's cutting off the wicked—but Job added that God in His omnipotence cuts off *both* the guilty and the guiltless, and thus He is unjust.

As Job spoke about God's wisdom and power, he seemed to say, "I know as much about Him as you do." By asking, "Who has defied Him without harm?" (9:4*b*), Job affirmed that man cannot challenge God and get away with it—and yet soon after that, Job challenged God! He spoke of God's might: He removes and overturns mountains (9:5), shakes the earth (9:6), darkens the sun and stars (9:7), stretches out the heavens (9:8*a*), tramples the waves of the sea[8] (9:8*b*), and creates the constellations—the Bear (the Big Dipper) in the north, Orion in the south, Pleiades in the east and west, and "the chambers of the south" (i.e., southern constellations) (9:9). He does great things that cannot be searched out or fully comprehended, and wondrous works that cannot be numbered (9:10); thus Job ironically quotes Eliphaz (5:9). God is incomprehensible: "Were He to pass by me, I would not see Him" (9:11). (Is Job alluding to Eliphaz's dream of a spirit passing by his face?) No one can keep God from snatching someone away, and no one can force God to answer the question, "What art Thou doing?" (9:

---

8. "Tramples down the waves" can be understood as "treads on the back of," thus referring to the sea dragon of Ugaritic mythology.

12). He is all-powerful and therefore sovereign and irresistible. How can man be righteous before such a God?

b. *God's arbitrariness* (9:13-24). Job had spoken of God's anger (9:5) and he returned to it again by stating, "God will not turn back His anger" (9:13). Then he added, "Beneath Him crouch the helpers of Rahab." The reference is to the Babylonian creation myth in which Marduk defeated Tiamat and then captured her helpers. God in His anger and power was able to conquer all the forces of evil, real and mythical. Rahab is another name for Tiamat, and for Leviathan, mentioned earlier (7:12). Rahab is also mentioned elsewhere in the Bible (Job 26:12; Psalms 87:4; 89:10; Isa 30:7; 51:9).

How could Job possibly plead his cause before such an angry, almighty God, or choose words for his defense (9:14)? Even if he were right (literally, just or righteous), he could not plead with Him; his only hope would be to implore the mercy of God, his Judge (9:15). Or if God were to respond to Job, he doubted that God would even listen to him (9:16).[9] The reason God would not listen to insignificant Job is that God seemed to be bent on destroying him (9:17-18): He bruised him with a tempest (Job's suffering is likened to his being buffeted in a storm), multiplied his wounds without cause (like an enemy attacking him), withheld his breath (cf. 7:15), and filled him with bitterness (cf. 7:11).

In both strength and justice, God is supreme. "If it is a matter of power, behold, He is the strong one! And if it is a matter of justice, who can summon [me]?" (9:19).[10] The first part of this verse looks back at God's power described in 9:13-18, and the second part looks ahead to God's justice discussed in 9:20-24. "Since God is supreme in power and subject to no court, man has no grounds on which to contend with him."[11] In either case—

---

9. Andersen suggests that Job was saying in 9:15b, "I *won't* appeal to my Judge by mercy," as Bildad had suggested (8:5). But it seems unwarranted to add a negative in 9:15b. Then Andersen deletes the negative (9:16b), (Francis I. Andersen, *Job: An Introduction and Commentary*, p. 147).
10. The NASB, following the Septuagint, has "who can summon Him?" but the Hebrew has "who can summon me?"
11. Marvin H. Pope, *Job*, p. 72.

48

whether a show of strength or a case of justice—Job felt that he could not possibly win.

God is so overwhelming, Job argued, that he was afraid he would become confused and witness in court against himself (9: 20)! Thus even though he was guiltless (the word is "blameless," already seen frequently in the book [e.g., 1:1, 8; 8:20, where it is translated as "of integrity"]), Job said he would not have a chance in court with God—He would declare him guilty. Job then blurted out his innocence in the simple affirmation, "I am guiltless!" (again the word "blameless"). "I do not take notice of myself," he continued. Job reached another point of despair. He did not even care about himself anymore; he hated his life (9: 21).

Job was saying, in essence, "What difference does it make whether I'm innocent or not?" "It is all one"; that is, it makes no difference. God destroys *both* "the guiltless and the wicked" (9:22). Job even went so far as to say that God, in His impersonal unconcern, mocks the innocent person who dies suddenly in a plague (9:23). In fact, God gives the earth to the wicked (they are the ones possessing the earth's wealth and dominating others) and covers (i.e., blindfolds) the judges so that they cannot be fair. Enraged at such inequities at the hand of God, Job cried out, "If it is not He, then who is it?" (9:24).

All this was in protest against the friends' notion that God blesses the good man and punishes the wicked. Job could not accept that view because, as he saw it, God destroys both. How can their concept of God's neat handing out of justice be reconciled with the facts of life? Job's own experience as a blameless person suffering at God's hand refuted their misconception of God's justice. Not that that consoled Job; although it refuted his assailants' ideas, it only added to his own despair.

c. *God's unfairness* (9:25—10:22). Such a deep despair led to another lament about his helpless condition. In this section Job stated that God would not acquit him (9:25-35), would not stop punishing him (10:1-7), would not leave him alone (10: 8-17), and would not let him die (10:18-22).

Reflecting on the brevity of life, Job observed that his days were going by quickly like a swift runner, like reed boats (with

49

wooden frames and sides of papyrus, the Egyptian speedboat of that day), and like a falcon that swoops on its prey (the peregrine falcon can reach a speed of 120 miles per hour in its downward air attack!)—the fastest on land, sea, and air (9:25-26).

Job knew that it would be futile for him to try to forget his problems and cheer up, because his pain would make him sad again and God would not possibly acquit him in court (9:27-28). Because he was considered by God (and his friends?) to be wicked, what good would it do to work at cleaning himself? Job said that even if he were to wash himself with soap[12] and his hands with lye, God was against him so much that He would plunge him into a cesspool of muck, so that even his clothes would despise him (9:29-31). God was determined to consider him guilty.

Aware of God's transcendence—"He is not a man"—Job sensed that he could never meet God in court. In no way could the gulf between God and man be bridged, not even by an arbiter. The word "umpire" may be translated "arbiter," and comes from a verb meaning "to argue, reason, or convict." The verb is elsewhere translated "argue" (13:3, 15), "reprove" (13:10; 40:2), and "reason" (Isa 1:18). The mediator was a person who could arbitrate a court case by listening to both sides ("lay his hand upon us both" [9:33]) and decide fairly, as a judge. Because no such person existed—who could be a higher authority than God Himself, who is involved in the case?—Job sensed that he was helpless.[13] His only hope was that God would voluntarily "remove his rod" of affliction and not frighten him (9:34). Only then could Job speak without fear of reprisal. But such thoughts were only wishful thinking. "I am not like that in myself" (9:35) means "that is not the way it is with regard to my case." God's rod was still on him. Job could not speak without fear of Him.

Because Job had no arbiter, he himself continued to challenge God and to speak on his own behalf—to be his own defense attorney. Next he bemoaned the fact that God would not

12. Not "snow," as in the NASB.
13. Of course Christ as the God-man, God incarnate, did become the Mediator between God and man (1 Tim 2:5), but it is wrong to assume that Job had a glimpse of Christ here.

stop punishing him (10:1-7). He wanted to know why God, knowing that he was not culpable, continued to punish him.

Job had said that he despised his life (9:21); now he repeated the thought, "I loathe my own life" (10:1). What was there to live for in such a dire condition? He had considered the alternative of forgetting his complaint and trying to be happy (9:27), but now he decided to do the opposite: to give "full vent to [his] complaint" and voice the bitterness he felt inside (10:1). The clause "I will say to God" (10:2a) indicates what Job would say if he had the opportunity. In this rehearsal of his speech before God, Job indicated that he would begin with an outright order, "Do not condemn me," and the insistence, "Let me know why Thou dost contend with me" (10:2).

Job challenged God by asking several questions. By his first question, he implied that God was wrong to oppress and reject him, His own creation, while favoring the wicked (10:3). "Is God enjoying the cat and mouse game? Is he like a capricious potter who makes pots just for the perverse pleasure of smashing them?"[14]

Job likened God to a man who looks harshly and intently for the faults of others (10:4), and to a man with a limited lifespan, who must seek out Job while He has the chance and must search out some sin for which He can hold him reprehensible (10:5-6). Job's implication was that because God is not man, He should not act as if He were. Then Job reaffirmed his innocence, "I am indeed not guilty." And yet God, aware of his guileless condition, continued to oppress him (10:7).

Next Job complained that God would not leave alone His own creation (10:8-17). Why should He lavish such creative work and providential care on Job only to destroy him and be angry with him? God fashioned him, so why should He destroy him (10:8)? God made him like a pot out of clay, so why should He smash him to dust again (10:9)? God caused Job to be conceived and develop in the womb—an intricate process like the curdling of milk into cheese; He had knitted (or woven)[15] to-

---

14. L. D. Johnson, *Israel's Wisdom: Learn and Live*, pp. 85-86.
15. This word (in Hebrew) is used only here and in Psalm 139:13, "Thou didst weave me in my mother's womb." It means "to weave or intertwine."

gether his bones and sinews, clothing him with skin and flesh (10:10-11). God gave him life, was loyal to him, and preserved his spirit by His care. After displaying such marvelous skill and loving concern, why should God consider him derelict? Why should He have made Job, all the while intending, as Job put it, "in Thy heart" to "take note of" him and not acquit him (10:12-14)?

In defiance, Job slashed out again at God. As he had stated earlier (9:22), he repeated his complaint that he would lose whether he was wicked or righteous (10:15). God would pursue him as if he were a lion being hunted. God's power would be demonstrated against him; more witnesses in court would be amassed against him; God's anger would increase against him (10:16-17). No wonder he sensed that life was nothing but one big hardship after another!

Then Job again expressed a desire for death (10:18-22). This section brings to mind Job's opening lamentation (chap. 3) and his earlier words (6:8-9). God had given great attention to him during his embryonic development only to hunt him down like a lion; what, then, was the purpose of even bringing him out of the womb? He would be better off if he had died in the womb and no one had ever seen him (10:18). He would like to be as if he had never been; he would have preferred to have been taken from the womb directly to the tomb (10:19)!

Because God had not let him be a miscarriage or a stillbirth, he longed for a little peace before death. If God would only let him alone so he could be cheerful (the same word for "cheerful" as in 9:27) for a little while before he would die, never to return (10:20-21). Job then called death a "land of darkness and deep shadow; the land of utter gloom as darkness itself, of deep shadow without order, and which shines as the darkness" (10:21-22). Here four different words for darkness are amassed to depict the horrible prospect of death, which is envisioned by Job as better than life with its miseries. In Sheol, even the shining is but darkness. Thus far, each of Job's speeches has ended on a gloomy note, with reference to death (3:21-22; 7:21; 10:21-22).

5

Arguing with God

5. Zophar's first speech (chap. 11)

Zophar was infuriated with Job for talking as he did. Job's claim to innocence and his wrestling with God brought a harsh, vicious retort from Zophar. Eliphaz and Bildad were certainly not tender, but Zophar's rude, insensitive spirit far surpassed theirs.

a. *His rebuke of Job's words* (11:1-6). Zophar was angered (1) because Job was so talkative ("Shall a multitude of words go unanswered, and a talkative man be acquitted?" [11:2]), (2) because Job was scoffing ("Shall your boasts silence men? And shall you scoff and none rebuke?" [11:3]—i.e., "You can't get away with such talk, Job"), (3) because Job was justifying himself ("You have said, 'My teaching is pure, and I am innocent in your eyes,' " [11:4]), and (4) because Job was ignorant of God (11:5-6).

In verses 5 and 6 Zophar sarcastically wished God *would* answer Job (cf. 9:3, 16). Then God would speak *against* Job, not for him. And God would "show you the secrets of wisdom! For sound wisdom has two sides"; that is, "True wisdom is beyond you."[1] You would see, Job, how stupid you are. In fact, God is letting you off easy. You are getting less punishment than you deserve; God is being nice to you!

b. *His praise of God's wisdom* (11:7-12). Whereas Eliphaz and Bildad had expounded God's inviolable justice, Zophar elaborated on God's inscrutable wisdom. The depths and extremities of God—His infinity—are beyond man's reach in all dimensions: higher than heaven, deeper than Sheol, longer than the earth, and wider than the sea (11:7-9). Although this is true theologically, Zophar's application of it to Job in the fol-

---

1. Literally, "double, folded over, two-sided," and therefore thick, difficult to penetrate.

lowing verses is wrong. Zophar agreed with Job's statement that no one can restrain God (11:10; cf. 9:12), but disagreed with Job's statement that God does not know the difference between the guilty and the innocent (11:11; cf. 9:22).

Zophar's stress on God's unfathomable wisdom, however, involved Zophar in a contradiction. For if God's ways are unknowable, how could Zophar know that God was overlooking some of Job's sin?

To stress Job's stupidity, Zophar quoted a proverb, "An idiot will become intelligent when the foal of a wild donkey is born a man" (11:12). In other words, the chances of an idiot's[2] becoming wise are as meager as the chances of a wild donkey's giving birth to a human being. The proverb graphically depicts stupidity, for wild donkeys were considered to be very stupid animals, more so than domesticated donkeys.

c. *His plea for Job's repentance* (11:13-20). Like Eliphaz and Bildad, Zophar assumed Job's sin and recommended that he repent. According to Zophar, three steps to being restored are proper conduct ("direct your heart right [11:13]), prayer ("spread out your hand to Him" [11:13]), and renunciation of sin ("put [iniquity] far away, and do not let wickedness dwell in your tents" [11:14]). If Job would meet those conditions—which heartlessly assumed that Job was living in sin and not in prayer—God would bless him with a clear conscience, steadfastness, confidence (11:15), no remembrance of trouble (11:16), joy (11:17; cf. Job's comment about darkness [10:22]), hope, rest (11:18), no disturbance, popularity, and leadership (11:19).

In concluding their speeches, all three friends promised restored blessing if Job would recant, but Bildad had ended his speech by saying the wicked will be destroyed (8:22) and then Zophar rounded off his terse, merciless tirade with a similar reminder-warning: "The eyes of the wicked will fail, and there will be no escape for them; and their hope is to breathe their last"[3] (11:20). Hardly any words could have been more biting.

2. Literally, "a man who is hollowed out," implying one who is empty in the head! One wonders if this proverb should apply to Zophar, rather than to Job.
3. Literally, "their hope is the breathing out of their life-spirit."

Several times already Job had expressed his longing to die—but in a strange twist Zophar made it appear that even such a death-wish was proof of sin!

6. *Job's first reply to Zophar* (chaps. 12—14)

The sources of authority on which the three counselors had based their argumentations would presumably leave Job silent. Who could refute someone else's dream? Who could argue with forefathers who are no longer alive? Who could debate with the infinite wisdom of God Himself? And yet Job was not to be silenced so easily. In his response in chapters 12—14, he castigated his friends and their view of God, turned once again to challenge God, but then again sunk into dejection over the death of man.

Half of his words were addressed to the friends (12:1—13:19) and half to God (13:20—14:22). After hearing the repetitious stand of all three men, he rose to a new height of frustration: though he rejected their rigid view of cause-and-effect justice, he had no way of accounting for what he observed about God's apparent injustice ("my eye has seen all this [13:1]). It brought to his mind again the desire to confront God with His injustice and demand an answer from Him.

a. *Job repudiated his friends* (12:1—13:19). Job sarcastically acknowledged their alleged wisdom. "Truly then you are the people, and with you wisdom will die" (12:2). He was not about to let them call him stupid and place him below them on the I.Q. scale. After all, he was a wise man of the East, too. In fact, he cleverly attacked their supposed monopoly on wisdom by pointing out that their views were common knowledge—everybody knows what they have said (12:3).[4]

However, their inflexible approach to justice—that God always blesses the upright—does not fit the facts. Job illustrated his point in several ways. First, he cited his own case. In the past he had called on God and he was just and blameless, yet God had let him be laughed at (12:4). His three advisers, who were

---

4. Referring, perhaps, to what they had said about God's providential care (5:9-10), His judgment on the wicked (8:13-19), and His infinity (11:7-9).

"at ease," thought nothing of making fun of unfortunate sufferers "whose feet slip" (12:5).

Second, he mentioned the case of destroyers (or better, robbers) and God-haters who prosper and are secure (12:6). Third, he noted that even animals know that calamities come from God's hand (12:7-9). By telling Zophar ("you" [12:7-8] is singular) to learn from animals, birds, earth creatures, and fish, Job was no doubt replying to Zophar's uncouth comment about Job's being more stupid than a wild donkey (11:12). Not only does God cause all things, but all life is in God's hands (12:10; cf. 10:12). By those three examples, Job tested his three friends' ideas, just as the ear tests words and the mouth tastes food (12:11).

"Wisdom is with aged men, with long life is understanding" (12:12), contradicts what Job had been saying. Therefore, he may be quoting the three counselors, and the verse should be in quotation marks and introduced by "You say."[5] Or the verse may be worded as a question ("Is wisdom with aged men . . .?") or as a sarcastic comment like 12:2.

At any rate, it is a refutation of Bildad's assertion that the source of wisdom is age (8:8). Job then recounted numerous instances of God's "wisdom and might," His "counsel and understanding" (12:13).[6] Job was saying, in effect, "You say that God is wise and powerful? I certainly know that. But His power and knowledge reveal the opposite of a clear, retributive justice, which you three are advocating. Added to my experience, the case of wicked robbers, and the experience of animals is a fourth illustration: many kinds of leaders are destroyed by God." "In hymnic majesty Job enumerates these outrageous acts of God as the true signs of his mysterious wisdom and spectacular power."[7]

God's destructive powers are irreversible. If He tears down, "it cannot be rebuilt," and if He imprisons someone, he cannot escape (12:14). When He holds back waters, there is drought,

5. Robert Gordis, *The Book of God and Man: A Study of Job,* p. 184.
6. If 12:12 is a quotation, then 12:13 would be understood as introduced by "But I say."
7. Norman C. Habel, *The Book of Job* (New York: Cambridge U., 1975), p. 64.

56

and if He releases the waters they flood the earth (12:15). Captives and captors alike are both under His control (12:16). He conquers, puts down, and reverses the fortunes of counselors, judges, kings, priests, "the secure ones" (i.e., well-established officials), "the trusted ones, elders, nobles, and the strong (12: 17-21)—those who are "the very foundations of justice and order in government, court and temple."[8] In addition to being wise and powerful over individual leaders, God is also sovereign over entire nations. He makes them great[9] and destroys them; He spreads them out (i.e., He causes their territory to extend) and leads them away (as captives).

All the above-mentioned human leaders are supposed to give light and security to others by their counsel and leadership. But in contrast to God, they are in darkness. Only He can reveal mysteries from the darkness and bring to light what is in the deep darkness (12:22). (Is this an answer to Zophar's question "Can you discover the depths of God?" [11:7]. If so, Job's response is that he cannot comprehend the infinite ways of God, but neither can Zophar! If man is ever to understand anything of what is incomprehensibly dark, God must take the initiative in revealing it to him.)

In contrast to His revelatory powers is God's ability to darken. Job said that God can deprive chiefs of their intelligence, even giving them such confusion that they stagger in the wasteland,[10] grope in the darkness, and stagger[11] like drunken men (12:24-25). What a picture of the directionless and unintelligible stupor of leaders who are objects of God's destructive powers.

And how cleverly Job demolished his counselors' counsel: If their theological system were followed, then all the world's authorities ought to be blessed by God. But history destroys that logic, as Job has just shown (12:13-25). *chap 13 begins*

Continuing his disavowal of the ash-heap advisers, Job repudiated their worth (13:1-5) and their competence to represent

8. Ibid., p. 68.
9. The verb "to make great" is an Aramaic word meaning "to cause to grow tall." The same verb was used by Bildad of reeds that grow tall (8:11).
10. The word "wasteland" is the word rendered "formless" (Gen 1:2), in describing the earth's chaos before God's creative work (Gen 1:3-31).
11. The word "stagger" is used in both 12:24 and 12:25.

God (13:6-12). Those repudiations are followed by his preparing to present his case to God (13:13-19).

Job backed up his words about God's mighty—even arbitrary—ways with the authority of his own observations. He was not going on hearsay or relaying on some misconstrued secondhand report. "My eye has seen all this, my ear has heard and understood it" (13:1). His senses of sight and sound had enabled him to discern with clarity God's actions and words. His knowledge of God thus exceeded the indiscernible form in Eliphaz's dream (4:16) and the indirect tradition of past generations to which Bildad appealed (8:8). Job was not to be outdone! He knew about God's character—and he knew it personally![12]

Therefore, he told them in no uncertain terms that he was their equal. Though they pretended to possess superior knowledge of God's ways, he knew what they knew (13:2a). Not about to be belittled, he affirmed with the confidence of one who knows he is right, "I am not inferior to you" (13:2b), repeating, for emphasis, his earlier words (12:3). Although outnumbered, he was not to be outargued.

Job "would speak to the Almighty"; he wanted "to argue[13] with God" (13:3). That would be far better than disputing with the three counselors. Presumably, if God would only talk with him, some explanation for his agony might be forthcoming; it certainly was not coming from the mouths of his self-appointed judges. Because they were representing him falsely, Job would have to be his own attorney.

After all, Job said, they "smear with lies . . . [and] are all worthless physicians" (13:4). Literally, Job said, "You are plasterers of lies," meaning that they "conceal what is wrong in God's control of the world by covering it over with a layer of lies"[14] about his own character. Physicians are supposed to possess the ability to diagnose and to prescribe; therefore, their failure to do so makes them "worthless." Likewise, persons who visit a grieving friend are useless if their words fail to console.

12. However, cf. 42:5.
13. The word "argue" is the verb from which comes "umpire" or "arbiter" (9:33). It suggests a legal disputation.
14. Victor E. Reichert, *Job*, p. 61.

Then with cutting wit, Job lashed out: "O that you would be completely silent, and that it would become your wisdom!" (13:5). Not only were they liars perverting the facts and physicians unable to help, but also they were fools whose words were exposing their ignorance. Although they professed to be wise, their talk revealed the opposite. Therefore, they could be considered wise if they would revert to the week-long silence of their first arrival.

As Job then rejected their competence to represent God (13:6-12), he again used legal terminology. "Please hear my argument" (13:6a) was a request for them to be silent while he presented his court case. "Listen to the contentions of my lips" (13:6b) was a plea for attention to the argumentations of his lawsuit.

Then Job addressed several questions to the three men. The Hebrew words "for God" and "for Him" (13:7) are at the beginning of the lines and thus are emphatic. The thought, then, is this: Is it for *God*, for His sake, that you speak wickedly, and is it for *His* benefit that you talk deceitfully about me? How unthinkable that God, the holy, righteous One, could be defended by unholy, unrighteous argumentations! "Will you show partiality for Him?" (13:8a) Job then asked. How unthinkable that the impartial God would benefit from and side with their partiality! The question "Will you contend for God?" (13:8b) also has "for God" in the emphatic position at the beginning. How unthinkable that lying fools could serve as God's defense attorneys!

In fact, when God examines[15] them, their deceit will be revealed. They may be able to deceive man, but not God (13:9). Because of their secret partiality, they will be reproved (13:10). The word "reprove" is the word rendered "argue" in 13:6, 15. Here it means "convict." Later, they actually were reproved by God, convicted by Him of the error of their views (42:7-8). Thinking they were defending God, they were really defending only their view about God. Reichert makes a helpful observation: "Note also the paradox of Job's spiritual torment. He can deny God's justice and yet affirm His moral perfection and right-

15. The word "examines" (13:9) is the same word used earlier by Eliphaz (5:27), "we have investigated it."

eous indignation against those who by flattery offer false testimony on His behalf."[16]

As Johnson puts it, "He who doubts God's concern for justice is at the same time confident that God is just!"[17]

Job suggested by a question that they, when examined by God, would be terrified[18] by His majesty (13:11). The self-hired attorneys seeking to defend God will be defenseless when God in His majestic, penetrating ways turns to examine and convict them.

Job then summarized their incompetence by stating that their "memorable sayings are proverbs of ashes" and that their "defenses are defenses of clay" (13:12). What *they* thought were maxims worthy of being remembered were actually as worthless as ashes. One can almost imagine Job gesturing to the pile of ashes around him as he denigrated the three men's proverbs built on a perversion of the facts. Attempting to defend God at Job's expense, they entrenched themselves behind arguments that were like fortresses or walls made of mud or clay. Ashes suggest worthlessness, and clay suggests weakness. Who would immemorialize ashes, and who would be safe from an enemy behind a clay wall?

Job then prepared to present his case to God (13:13-19), as he had said he longed to do (13:3).

Twice in the chapter he requested that they be silent (13:5, 13), and twice he requested that they listen (13:6, 17). Fearlessly, he was ready to speak out and suffer the consequences: "Be silent before me so that I may speak; then let come on me what may" (13:13).

The next verse continues to express that awareness of risk: "Why should I take my flesh in my teeth, and put my life in my hands?" (13:14). Taking his flesh in his teeth meant risking his life. An animal that carries the flesh of its prey in its mouth risks losing it, because other animals, seeing it, would desire to seize it. Job, then, knew that he was putting himself in a dangerous

16. Reichert, p. 62.
17. L. D. Johnson, *Out of the Whirlwind: The Major Message of Job,* pp. 34-35.
18. The word "terrify" was also used earlier by Job (7:14; 9:34), and will be used again (13:21).

position by speaking directly to God, but he was determined to take the risk, even to the point of losing his own life.

"Though He slay me, I will hope in Him" (13:15a) is a beautiful expression of faith, widely quoted and familiar to many Christians. However, the rendering is based on marginal notes in the Hebrew rather than on the accepted Hebrew text. The word "Though" should read "Behold" and the words "in Him" should be replaced by the word "not," so that the verse reads, "Behold, He will slay me; I do not have hope." Not only is that a more accurate rendering of the Hebrew, but it also correlates better with the preceding verse. Job fully anticipated that his self-defense would result in his being killed by God. But he was more concerned for maintaining justice than for maintaining his life: "Nevertheless I will argue my ways before Him."[19]

If Job could argue his case with God, that, he said, would "be my salvation" (13:16a). "Salvation" here no doubt means his vindication. He knew that God might kill him for his brashness; he was aware that he was taking his life in his hands. But he was certain that God, being just, would acquit him. He could dare to challenge God because of his clear conscience, for "a godless [irreligious] man may not come before His presence" (13:16b).

Again Job requested careful attention to his words (13:17), his readiness to appear in court, and the certainty of his acquittal. When he said, "I have prepared my case" (13:18a), he meant that he had marshaled his arguments, like a diligent lawyer carefully preparing his presentation.[20] By saying, "I know that I will be vindicated [literally, justified]" (13:18b), Job meant that he would win the case. He was confident of the outcome. It is a stroke of boldness, in contrast to his previous words of despair: "I know that Thou wilt not acquit me" (9:28b).

By asking "Who will contend with me?" (13:19a), Job was once more boldly affirming the impossibility of anyone's bringing honest charges of guilt against him. If someone, including even God, could do so, then—and only then—would he be silent and die.

19. Literally, "I will present my case [or, defend my ways] to His face."
20. "To prepare" means "to marshal an army for battle."

Job was taking his life in his teeth, but because of his confidence that he could win his legal battle, he was willing to take the risk. Thus far in this speech (12:1—13:19), Job has moved from a daring, head-on repudiation of his alleged consolers, through a delineation of the arbitrary, mysterious ways of God, to a bold readiness for a direct confrontation with God. The next nine verses include that presentation of his case in court.

b. *Job presented his case to God* (13:20-28). Thus far in each reply to the friends, Job addressed God. In responding to Eliphaz, Job turned to God (7:12-21). In replying to Bildad, Job spoke to God (9:28-33; 10:2-19). And in his rejoinder to Zophar, he approached God (13:20—14:22).

He requested two things from the Lord: that He remove His hand from him and that He not let His dread terrify him (13:20-21). In a court case it would be only fair that the defendant not be intimidated. The second request may be an allusion to Eliphaz's frightening dream (4:12-21).[21]

Job then offered to meet God in court as either defendant or plaintiff. "Then call, and I will answer; or let me speak, then reply to me" (13:22). Job was so concerned that God communicate with him that he did not care who spoke first. Either way, he was ready.

Having received no response from God, Job proceeded to speak first. He asked God to enumerate his sins (13:23), using three different words for sin. But even then, no response came from God. Only silence. Job wanted his companions to be silent, but they continued to talk. Job wanted God to speak, but He remained silent.

This silence from the heavens led Job to ask why God would hide His face and treat him like an enemy (13:24).[22] How could God torment the helpless: "Wilt Thou cause a driven leaf [i.e., a leaf blown by the wind] to tremble?" And how could He be concerned with troubling the insignificant: "Wilt Thou pursue the dry chaff?" (13:25).

---

21. Charles W. Carter, "The Book of Job," in *The Wesleyan Bible Commentary*, ed. Charles W. Carter, vol. 2 (Grand Rapids: Eerdmans, 1968), p. 88.
22. Several times Job spoke of God's treating him as an enemy (6:4; 7:20; 13:24; 16:9, 12, 13).

God's silence apparently caused Job soon to forget his line of defense, for Job said hardly anything about his innocence. Disappointed and frustrated that God would not appear with him in court, Job flared further accusations at God for unfairly hitting him when he was down. In fact, Job then told God that He wrote bitter charges (i.e., unfair accusations) against him, and also was unjustly punishing him for sins Job committed decades before as a young person (13:26).

By declining to interact with Job, God was treating him like a prisoner, boxing him in and making it impossible for him to solve his dilemma. God, Job claimed, put his feet in stocks, "chains," watched every move he made, and branded his feet[23] so that He could easily track Job by his unusual footprints.

Job then began to sink back into despair as he expressed the words, "[He][24] is decaying like a rotten thing, like a garment that is moth-eaten" (13:28). Job felt that God was unjust in imprisoning the steps of one who was feeble, decaying, and worthless.

The boldness with which Job began his self-defense was suddenly burst by God's silence. Like a sick man who thinks he has strength to sit up in bed but suddenly falls back in weakness, Job rose with a dash of daring only to be immediately swept back to his feelings of unfair persecution at God's hands. This led to further depths of despair, expressed in chapter 14.

c. *Job despaired of hope* (chap. 14). In his sudden shift of mood, Job turned from an audacious overconfidence in his belief that he could win his court case to a melancholy lament over the brevity of life (14:1-6), the finality of death (14:7-17), and the absence of hope (14:18-22). Earlier, he had voiced his willingness to risk his life in order to argue his case (chap. 13). Now he sensed that he had lost in his gamble with God and life (chap. 14). How can one win his case if the defendant will not heed the subpoena to appear in court? Job languished back to a melancholy elegy over life's futility and death's certainty.

23. "Thou dost set a limit for the soles of my feet" (13:27) is better rendered "Thou dost brand the soles of my feet."
24. "And he" is the original reading, not "While I am." The "he" refers to man oppressed by God.

By stating that man "is born of woman" (14:1), Job pointed to man's frailty. Because woman is frail, what comes from her is also frail. Added to this impotence of the human race is the fact that man is "short-lived" (literally, "short of days")[25] and full of turmoil.[26] This curtailed existence is likened to a flower that blossoms with promise but soon withers, and to a mere shadow[27] that "does not remain" (14:2) in one place because of the earth's continual movement.

"Thou also dost open Thine eyes on him" to scrutinize a feeble, fleeting creature for punishment. Job had called God the "watcher of men" (7:20). Job added here that God brings man "into judgment with Thyself." Job realized that instead of his being able to accuse God of wrongdoing, God was judging *him*. And again, this seemed unfair. Why should God judge such a defenseless creature?

Job clamored over the hopelessness of ever being able to be made clean before the bar of such a God: "Who can make the clean out of the unclean? No one!" (14:4). This is reminiscent of his earlier words (9:30-31) and is repeated by Bildad later (25:4).

Not only are man's days few; they are also "determined" (i.e., their number is fixed by God), and "the number of his months is with Thee" (i.e., God knows man's allotted months [14:5]). What is more, God has set limits beyond which man cannot go. The word "limits" means "something cut" and then "something prescribed," possibly meaning here a prescribed limit of time, not a geographical limit. When man's predetermined days are up, he cannot live one day beyond that set limit.

Because man is so hemmed in and his days so ephemeral, the least God could do would be to "turn [His] gaze from him that he may rest" (14:6*a;* cf. 7:19; 10:20). Job longed for a respite from God's cruel watchfulness over him so that like a hired hand he could find some rest at the end of his day of labor (14:6*b*).

25. Job had already spoken of life's brevity (7:7-10; 9:25-26; 10:20*a*).
26. The word "turmoil," already used by Job (3:17, where it is translated "raging"; 3:26), means "agitation."
27. The words in Hebrew for "flower" and "shadow" are similar in sound: *tsits* and *tsāh*. This alliteration, a typical Hebrew device, would make an impression on the hearer and reader and help them recall the words.

Brevity, toil, and God's relentless scrutiny are all suggested in this verse.

Turning from the futility of life to the futility of death (14: 7-17), Job made a contrast between man and trees and then a comparison between man and water. A tree, when cut down, may sprout again and its shoots flourish. And even though its roots may grow old or its stump may decay in the dry soil from lack of water, the tree detecting the presence of water nearby "will flourish and put forth sprigs [i.e., it will bud] like a [new] plant" (14: 9). When man dies, however, he lies prostrate, he expires, and when he is buried no one sees him (14:10). The contrast seemed unfair to Job. Why should there be more hope for a mere tree than for man?

In the comparison, man is likened to water that evaporates from the sea (the word means a lake) and to a river that dries up. "So man lies down and does not rise" (14:12a). He is utterly extinct, with death considered final and permanent. Job then likened death to a sleep from which man cannot be awakened or aroused "until the heavens be no more" (14:12b). Because the heavens were considered permanent, Job spoke hypothetically: "Even if the heavens could pass away, men would still not awake from death."

Though having just denied the possibility of resurrection, Job then reflected on what it might mean. If resurrection were possible, he would look on his time in Sheol as a time of hiding. Sheol, the locality or condition of the dead, was where man would either suffer or rest.

In a flash of hope, Job longed for the possibility that Sheol would become a hiding place, that God would conceal him (lay him away in security) until His wrath would return (i.e., until His wrath would no longer be extended to Job). If only God would set a limit for his time in Sheol (just as He had set a limit for his days on earth) and then remember him (14:13). Job seemed willing to endure the mysterious regions of Sheol if that would be the means of relief from divine wrath and the step toward reconciliation with God and resurrection by God.

"If a man [a strong man] dies, will he live again?" (14:14a). By this inquiry Job reached out wistfully and longingly for the

65

possibility of life after death, thus voicing man's universal desire. "Such is the lingering desire of life in the bosom of man in the severest trials, and the darkest hours. . . ."[28] With that faint prospect of resurrected life, Job was willing to wait out "the days of [his] struggle" in this life "until [his] change [i.e., relief] comes" (14:14). The word "struggle" is literally "warfare" or "service," suggesting that Job looked on life as compulsory military service or forced labor. The word "relief" is used of one group of soldiers replacing and thus relieving another group.

Reverting again to judicial court proceedings, Job was sure that in the future God would call him to court and that he would answer the summons. He was certain that God would someday "long for the work of [His] hands" (14:15; cf. 10:3, where Job referred to himself as "the labor of [God's] hands"). The words "long for" render the Hebrew word that means "to be or become pale like silver." God, Job asserted, would be pale with a deep emotional longing for Job while he was in Sheol.

"For now," which begins 14:16, probably should be rendered "Surely then," referring to the time when God would long for and call for Job. In this brief rhapsody of anticipated fellowship with God, Job delighted in that time when He would "number [his] steps" but would not keep watch over his sin (14:16). God would then be the "watcher of men" (7:20) but for a different purpose—that of providential care, not dogged scrutiny of sin (cf. 14:6). And Job's transgression would be "sealed up in a bag" (out of sight as evidence against him), and God would "wrap up" (cover or plaster over) his "iniquity" (14:17).

Gathering still more metaphors from nature,[29] Job referred to the falling mountains crumbling away, the rock moving from its otherwise stationary position, water wearing away stones, and torrents washing away the dust (soil) of the earth as portraits of the way God destroys man's hope (14:18-19). The Hebrew word for "man" is again the word meaning man in his weakness. Even the faint hope that frail man may conjure is gradually and persistently washed away.

28. Albert Barnes, *Notes, Critical, Illustrative, and Practical, on the Book of Job*, 1:272.
29. Flower (14:2), shadow (14:2), tree (14:7-9), water of a lake (14:11), river (14:11).

Not only are man's hopes dashed, but also his very existence is overpowered forever[30] by God so that he departs (or, is gone). God also changes man's appearance, a reference no doubt to the change in man's face made by death. The countenance that was flush with life is now pallid from the touch of death. God sends man away—away from family, friends, possessions, prestige—to a shadowy existence in distant Sheol (14:20).

Death removes man's knowledge of events on earth. It does not permit man the parental joy of seeing his sons honored, nor does it allow him the opportunity of sympathizing with his children in their problems (14:21). Man knows only his own misery. His pain is both physical ("his body [literally, flesh] pains him") and mental ("he mourns only for himself") (14:22). The body feels the gnawing of corruption in the grave and the soul mourns in conscious misery.

Job ended this speech on a sullen note of death, a morose tone of despondency. Each speech by Job in this first round concluded with a mournful reference to death. In this final speech of the first round Job had refuted the worth of his friends' counsel, acknowledged the arbitrary power of God, dared to present his case boldly and directly to God, had his hopes dashed by God's unexplainable silence, longed for the possibility of postdeath life, and succumbed to hopeless despair, for only death awaited him. These

> transitions, of course, are sudden, apparently abrupt, sometimes seemingly contradictory; and in this lies much of the dramatic power of the unknown author of this wondrous production. Imagine the aged mourner lying on the earth,—sackcloth on his body, and ashes on his head, his "face soiled with weeping," his "horn in the dust," the "shadow of death upon his eyelids"—now cursing his day, now sinking in despondency, now rising in hope, now humbled in prayer, now patient in tribulation.[31]

---

30. The verb "overpower" occurs only here, in 15:24, and Ecclesiastes 4:12. It means "to overcome with irresistible power." "Forever" means "continually or uninterruptedly."

31. Taylor Lewis, "Spirituality of the Book of Job as Exhibited in a Commentary on Chapter XIV, Examined in Connection with Other Passages," *Bibliotheca Sacra and Theological Review* 6 (August 1849): 502.

6

Ash-Heap Duel

C. THE SECOND CYCLE OF SPEECHES (chaps. 15—21)

In the second round of desert discourses, Eliphaz, Bildad, and Zophar clung tenaciously to their beliefs about suffering in relation to sin. The monotonous repetition with which they insisted on their views shows the reader their persistence and their inability to understand Job's dilemma.

One difference from the first round becomes evident in their second speeches (chaps. 15, 18, 20): The friends were less friendly and more fierce. Their disputations were more abusive, their argumentations less tolerant. Perturbed by Job's refusal to repent and his audacious confrontation with God, the three interlocutors attacked him with a venomously hostile spirit.

What is more, they no longer held out to Job the challenge to repent. The call to restoration as a means of once more acquiring the sunshine of God's blessing is noticeably absent in this second cycle.

The second round underscores the theme of the fate of the wicked, with each visitor stressing a slightly different aspect of the subject. Eliphaz said that the wicked are in distress and are endangered (chap. 15), Bildad spewed out the point that the wicked are ensnared and forgotten (chap. 18), and Zophar lambasted Job with the heartless observation that the wicked are shortlived and lose their wealth (chap. 20).

Further, each friend-turned-foe spoke insultingly to Job. In 15:8, Eliphaz challenged Job with the question "Do you think you're as smart as God?" Bildad hinted that Job was stupid and angry (18:2-4). And Zophar flared at Job with the implication that Job had insulted him (20:2-3). They were moving further and further away from the initial intention of their visit: to console. Their words, which should have been chosen carefully in order to fall smoothly like salve for the soul, became arrows of acrimony and spears of bitterness, injecting a maddening poison.

1. *Eliphaz's second speech* (chap. 15)

In his first speech, elderly Eliphaz had followed the decorum of the Middle East by speaking politely and indirectly, having been careful not to strike Job's wounded soul. In his second oration, Eliphaz abandoned such courtesy and "openly and sharply attacks Job with one dagger-thrust after another."[1] At first Eliphaz considered Job a righteous man temporarily chastened by God, but now Eliphaz saw him as a hardened sinner in arrogant rebellion against God.[2]

Eliphaz's second spiel divides into a rebuke of Job's attitude (15:1-16) and a reminder of the wicked man's fate (15:17-35).

a. *A rebuke of Job's attitude* (15:1-16). Eliphaz accused Job of irreverent talk (15:1-6) and of an assumed wisdom and purity (15:7-16). Caustically, Eliphaz asked, "Should a wise man answer with windy knowledge, and fill himself with the east wind? Should he argue with useless[3] talk, or with words which are not profitable?" (15:2-3). Job's hot-air talk disproved his claim to wisdom, for no wise man uses windy knowledge (a reminder of Bildad's reference to Job's words as a "mighty wind" [8:2]). Nor does a wise man fill himself (literally, his belly) with the sirocco, the dreaded, hot desert wind that blows from the east. Job's words were useless and unprofitable, as empty as wind and as violent as hot-air blasts from the desert.

Rather than fostering a reverent attitude toward God, Job, according to Eliphaz, did away with (literally, diminished or undermined) reverence (i.e., piety or fear of God), and actually hindered meditation (i.e., devotion) before God (15:4). Eliphaz continued his railing: "Your guilt [better, your iniquity] teaches your mouth." In other words, "Your sin causes you to speak irreverently against God. Your very words of boastful self-defense testify to the presence of inner sin."

1. Charles W. Carter, "The Book of Job," in *The Wesleyan Bible Commentary,* ed. Charles W. Carter, vol. 2 (Grand Rapids: Eerdmans, 1968), p. 93.
2. Marvin H. Pope, *Job,* p. 114.
3. "Useless" (without benefit) is used eleven times in the Old Testament, five times in Job and six times elsewhere.

The elder of the trio sought to free himself from hurling accusations at Job by observing that Job's own words condemned him and Job's own lips testified against him (15:6).

Eliphaz then assailed Job for assuming to be wise and pious. Again he began with several questions: "Were you the first man to be born, or were you brought forth before the hills? Do you hear the secret counsel of God, and limit wisdom to yourself?" (15:7-8). Eliphaz was saying, "Who does Job think he is—the oldest man on earth, and therefore the wisest? Does he think he, like wisdom, existed before the creation of the long-enduring mountains [cf. Prov 8:25]? Does he suppose he has access to God's secret counsels? Does he think only he is wise?"

Eliphaz's insinuations were unfair, for Job had claimed no such thing. He had simply claimed intelligence on a par with the three (12:3; 13:2). Job had asked, "Who does not know such things as these?" (12:3b) and had said, "What you know I also know" (13:2a). Now Eliphaz threw Job's claim back at him with two more questions: "What do you know that we do not know? What do you understand that we do not?" (15:9). Job had challenged their claim that wisdom accompanied only old age (12:12), so Eliphaz retorted with the affirmation that "both the gray-haired and the aged are among us, older than your father" (15:10). Job, though a mature man, should have respect for the wisdom of his elders. From Eliphaz's vantage point, Job's contesting of their theology was an inexcusable act of disrespect for the elderly.

Continuing to belittle Job with sarcastic questions, Eliphaz interrogated Job about his relationship to God. Eliphaz felt that Job's attitude toward the Lord was at least as wrong as his attitude toward his comforters. "Are the consolations of God too small for you, even the word spoken gently with you?" (15:11). That is, "Aren't you content with what God is doing for you?" By mentioning God's consolations—His acts of comfort—Eliphaz may have been subtly reminding Job of what Eliphaz had said in his first speech about God's ways (5:17-27). And the "word spoken gently" denoted Eliphaz's kind approach in his earlier discourse.

Then Eliphaz pulled this arrow of interrogation from his quiver of rhetoric: "Why does your heart carry you away? And why do your eyes flash, that you should turn your spirit against God, and allow such words to go out of your mouth?" (15:12-13). Eliphaz accused Job of letting his emotions control his reason and of venting his anger, but Eliphaz himself was guilty of irrational emotion. And he was wrong in alleging that Job had turned his spirit against God.

Sensing that Job did not assimilate what Eliphaz had said about man in his first talk, he repeated himself. Weak man is impure; and born of woman, he is unrighteous (15:14; cf. 4:17). God does not trust His angels, Eliphaz argued, and the heavens are not pure, so how can man be trusted by God or stand in moral purity before Him—man, who is "detestable" (a word meaning repulsive) and "corrupt" (a word meaning sour like milk, used only here and in Psalms 14:3; 53:3), and "who drinks iniquity like water" (15:15-16; cf. 4:18; 34:7). The clear implication is that *Job* is impure, unrighteous, detestable, and corrupt, and that he guzzles sin as naturally and intensely as if it were water. It is true that man is a corrupt sinner, but Eliphaz was wrong in assuming that Job's suffering stemmed from deliberate impiety.

b. *A reminder of the wicked man's fate* (15:17-35). These words by Eliphaz about the wicked and his coming punishments were designed to shock Job into repentance. As in his first speech to Job, so in his second speech also Eliphaz based his words on observation. "What I have seen I will also declare" (15:17) recalls his earlier, identical words "what I have seen" (4:8). Then Eliphaz sought to buttress his authority further by appealing to the wisdom of ancestors, as Bildad had done in his first appeal (8:8). Eliphaz was about to tell Job something wise men had told—traditions from their fathers, traditions that had not been hidden[4] (15:18) but had been passed on, traditions that foreigners had not adulterated with their philosophies (15:19). According to Eliphaz, Job, by rejecting such teaching, was showing his disdain for the elderly wise, he was rejecting tradition, he

4. This clause may mean that wise men have not hidden their fathers' traditions, or that the wise men's fathers have not hidden the traditions. Probably the former is to be preferred.

was blinding himself to the obvious, and he was associating with alien teachings. How foolish could Job be!

Verses 20-35 present the judgments and troubles that fall on the wicked because of their sin. Eliphaz was implying that Job, the wicked person, was experiencing some troubles then, with others to follow. Eliphaz stressed the inner turmoil confronting the one with a guilty conscience.

1. "The wicked man writhes in pain all his days" (15:20*a*). Job had said that in death his flesh pains him (14:22), but Eliphaz commented that the pain is not limited to death; it is experienced during one's entire lifetime! The Hebrew word rendered "writhes in pain" refers to a woman's labor pains, thus suggesting intense agony. The verb is also translated "brought forth" (15:7).

2. "Numbered are the years [literally, The number of years are] stored up for the ruthless" (15:20*b*). Job had spoken of his days and months' being determined (14:5), and Eliphaz referred to the same idea but mentioned that *years* are numbered. "Ruthless" means "terror-striking." How thoughtlessly unkind—and untrue—of Eliphaz to suggest that Job was a tyrant striking fear in other people.

3. "Sounds of terror are in his ears" (15:21*a*). One who strikes terror in others is himself terrified. Possibly this refers to imaginary sounds haunting his stricken conscience.

4. "While at peace the destroyer comes upon him" (15:21*b*). Again Eliphaz was brutally inconsiderate, for that very thing had happened to Job (1:13-19). The word for "destroyer" can be translated "robber"; Job himself had used the Hebrew word to illustrate the opposite of his disputers' contentions: "the tents of the destroyers prosper" (12:6).

5. "He does not believe that he will return from darkness" (15:22*a*). The meaning is that the sinner is tormented by his guilty conscience; he is always fearing that he may not awake from his sleep, or he is always dreading misfortune. This is the first of three times Eliphaz used the word "darkness" in this harangue.

72

6. "He is destined for the sword" (15:22b). "The wicked man feels he is marked out as the victim of violence."[5]

7. "He wanders about for food, saying, 'Where is it?' He knows that a day of darkness is at hand" (15:23). Fearful that he may become impoverished, the unrighteous man seeks to hunt and hoard food, anticipating his need for hiding because of his wrongdoing. For such a person, darkness stalks in the daytime.

8. "Distress and anguish terrify him, they overpower him like a king ready for the attack" (15:24). The sinner who has brought distress and anguish on others suffers the same in turn. Eliphaz threw back at Job the word "terrify," which the sufferer had used four times already. Job had said that God terrified him with Eliphaz's apparition-in-the-vision report (7:14), twice he had requested that God not terrify him (9:34; 13:21), and he had told the three counselors that God's majesty would terrify them (13:11). The word "overpower" had also been used before: Job had said that God overpowers man (14:20). Eliphaz pointed out that man's own anguish irresistibly overpowers him like a king with his armies amassed for attack.

Verses 25 and 26 introduce the reasons for the inner turmoils stated in verses 20-24. Verses 27 and 28 introduce other reasons for the judgments that follow (vv. 29-35). The pattern is as follows:

15:20-24   Judgments
15:25-26   Reasons for the judgments
15:27-28   Reasons for the judgments
15:29-35   Judgments

The man, Eliphaz contends, who "has stretched out his hand against God, and conducts himself arrogantly against the Almighty" (15:25) will suffer the agonizing torture of pain, fear, and guilt. The outstretched hand is a gesture of defiance. The words "conducts" and "arrogantly" are an intense form of the verb that means "to be strong" like a warrior. Eliphaz believed that Job was warring against God; again, this opinion is a twisting of Job's position that God was warring with *him* (7:20; 13:

5. Victor E. Reichert, *Job,* p. 76.

73

24). Furthermore, the elder counselor added, the wicked person "rushes headlong [literally, with a stiff neck, i.e., stubbornly] at Him with his massive shield" (15:26), an offensive attack with a thick shield for defense. Eliphaz had already accused Job of turning his spirit against God (15:13).

In addition to defiance against God, Job, according to Eliphaz, was guilty of self-indulgence: "He has covered his face with his fat, and made his thighs heavy with flesh" (15:27). In the Old Testament a chubby person symbolizes selfish luxury and spiritual insensitivity (Psalms 73:7; 119:70; Jer 5:28).[6] In addition, he proudly lived in ruined cities and rebuilt houses previously unoccupied, thus defying the curse on ruined sites (15:28; cf. Josh 6:26; 1 Kings 16:34).

Eliphaz moved from the inner anguish of a tormented conscience to the sins that account for such uneasiness: arrogant defiance against God and an attack against Him. Then he cited the sinner's "ostentatious luxury and brazen conduct,"[7] which were the basis for the judgments to follow in 15:29-35.

9. "He will not become rich, nor will his wealth endure; and his grain will not bend down to the ground" (15:29). Although the transgressor puts on an air of opulence through his gluttony, his affluence will not last. In fact, his corn will not be heavy with grain and thus will not droop to the ground.[8] His wealth will be taken away, and his farmland will not yield productive crops. Famine will be the result.

10. "He will not escape from darkness" (15:30a). The dreaded calamity (15:22-23) will come, and there will be no escape.

11. "The flame will wither his shoots, and by the breath of His mouth he will go away" (15:30b-c). His crops will be so dry that a fire will finish them off, with no possibility of their being rejuvenated like the tree of which Job spoke (14:7-8). God's

6. There is little basis for the view that the wicked smeared himself with grease to swim, as Hugh Anderson suggests ("The Book of Job," in *The Interpreter's One-Volume Commentary on the Bible*, ed. Charles M. Laymon [Nashville: Abingdon, 1971], p. 245).

7. H. H. Rowley, *Job*, p. 141.

8. The meaning of "his grain," occurring only here in the Old Testament, is difficult to determine. Another meaning is "his possessions" (in which case "bend down to" should be rendered "spread over").

breath (a subtle reference to the hot east wind?) will blow him and his possessions away.

12. "Let him not trust in emptiness, deceiving himself; for emptiness will be his reward. It will be accomplished before his time" (15:31-32a). To trust in emptiness (vanity) is to receive it in turn and come to a premature end. This illustrates Eliphaz's maxim, "those who sow trouble harvest it" (4:8).

13. "His palm branch will not be green. He will drop off his unripe grape like the vine, and will cast off his flower like the olive tree" (15:32b-33). These images from botany were given by Eliphaz to elaborate further on the loss of the wicked man's wealth. This promise of forthcoming affluence will not be fulfilled.

14. "The company of the godless is barren, and fire consumes the tents of the corrupt" (15:34). The "godless gang" (as the phrase may be rendered) will be as unproductive as a rock ("barren" was used earlier by Job [3:7]), and tents of bribers (the meaning of "corrupt") will go up in flames. Eliphaz again repeated previous points, adding very little new, for he had said that the tent-cord of the wicked will be plucked up (4:21) and Bildad had said that the tent of the wicked "will be no more" (8:22). Eliphaz may also have been mercilessly referring to Job's possessions, which had gone up in flames. The losses of the wicked are extensive.

15. "They conceive mischief and bring forth iniquity, and their mind prepares deception" (15:35). "Mischief" is "toil" or "trouble," to which man is born, as Eliphaz had said before (5:7). It may carry the idea of the womb, thus continuing the metaphor of childbirth. Trouble is conceived, iniquity is born, and the womb (not "mind") fashions deception. Although the godless are sterile as a rock (15:34), they do conceive trouble, give birth to iniquity, and develop deception in the womb. Eliphaz was going back to the judgment of self-deception (15:31). He had begun his listing of judgments by using the figure of chilbirth (writhing in labor pains [15:20]), and he concluded by going back to the same metaphor (15:34-35), perhaps alluding subtly to Job's initial obsequy, in which he wished he had never been born (3:3-10).

2. *Job's second reply to Eliphaz* (chaps. 16—17).

Outraged by Eliphaz's cruel harangue, Job retorted with scorn and bewailed his painful sense of isolation from God.

a. *Job's disgust—with his friends* (16:1-5). Locked in conflict in this ash-heap duel, Job again rejected the unwanted advice of his visitors. What Eliphaz had said was nothing new ("I have heard many such things"), and Job declared all three men "sorry comforters" (16:2). Some friends they were! They were so-called comforters (cf. Eliphaz's claim that his words spoke God's consolations [15:11]), but they brought only trouble. (The Hebrew word for "sorry" is translated as "mischief" [trouble] in the last sentence of Eliphaz's second speech [15:35].)

Bildad had called Job's words "a mighty wind" (8:2), and Eliphaz had indicted Job for having "windy knowledge" and for having filled his belly with the "east wind" (15:2). Therefore, Job in turn disavowed their proclamations as "windy words" (16:3).

Not comprehending why they should be so agitated over his efforts to get a hearing with God, he asked, "What plagues [literally, irritates] you that you answer [i.e., that you keep on replying]?" (16:3*b*). Later Zophar answered that question (20:2-3).

If their positions were reversed, Job postulated, he could speak as they were. He could compose words (i.e., string words together; or possibly, from the Ugaritic, pile up words) and shake his head at them as an act of mocking (16:4; cf. 2 Kings 19:21; Psalm 22:7). He could do far better than they were doing, for he could indeed strengthen people with his words (as Eliphaz admitted that Job had done previously [4:4]), and he could offer solace that would ease their pain.

b. *Job's distress—at the hand of God* (16:6-17). Job felt that he was not helped by his three comforters; nor could he help himself, for whether he spoke or was quiet, his pain was not assuaged (16:6).[9] In fact, his pain[10] had worn him out (16:7*a*).

His major concern, however, was not the crass invective of his

9. "What has left me?" may be read "it does not leave me."
10. The Hebrew for "He" may be rendered "it," referring to his pain. The context (16:6) seems to favor this.

self-claimed consolers, but the torment by God. Job pictured God as the One who deprived him of family and friends (16:7b) and shriveled him up, the Hebrew word for "shriveled" (used only here [16:8a] and in 22:16, where it is translated "snatched away") meaning "seized" or "grabbed." This evident affliction was seen by his friends as evidence of his having sinned, and his lean body, emaciated by disease, testified against him in the same way.

Job then depicted God as a savage beast, tearing him in anger, snarling at him, and glaring at him (literally, sharpening his eyes) (16:9)—indications of fierce hostility. Then, speaking of his companions, he said that they gaped at him (i.e., spoke derisively of him), treated him with contempt, and massed themselves against him like an army in close rank (16:10). Returning then to God's molestation, Job accused God of giving him over to ruffians (possibly meaning young, depraved urchins who ventured near the ash pile and may have besmirched Job disrespectfully), tossing him to the wicked (for maltreatment), shattering him while he was at ease, and shaking him by the neck (16:11-12). Job then compared God's vexations to the actions of an archer. The situation was as if God were using him for target practice (cf. 6:4; 7:20), surrounding him with arrows and then hitting him straight on, mercilessly splitting his kidneys and piercing his gall (16:12-13). Still another figure of speech was used—that of a warrior breaking through a wall, attacking first from one breakthrough and then another, and chasing him down (16:14). Job thus amassed a forceful collocation of word-pictures to portray the intensity of his emotional writhing and the helplessness of his pitiable condition.

As a result of God's violent assaults, Job was wearing sackcloth, indicative of mourning, and he had thrust his "horn in the dust" (16:15), the figure of a defeated animal. His face was red from his tears and his eyelids were darkened in color, both symptoms of grief (16:16). Yet he could not for a moment concede to his colleague's dogmas. His ordeal was simply unaccountable, for he had practiced no violence (negatively) and he said "my prayer is pure" (positively) (16:17). He had not acted wickedly toward others, and he had maintained a life of devotion before God, with pure motives and a clear conscience.

c. *Job's desire—for a representative in heaven* (16:18—17:2). This consciousness of his integrity before God spurred Job to desire a solution. By pleading that the earth not cover his blood (16:18*a*), he was asking that after his death the injustice he had undergone would be seen and vengeance executed (cf. Gen 4:10). "Let there be no resting place for my cry" (16:18*b*) means "may my plea for justice not be buried."

After speaking of the earth, Job referred to heaven, confident that there was a "witness" in heaven (someone who would testify and work on his behalf) and an "advocate" on high. Was Job appealing to the God whom he had just described so vociferously as his enemy? The context, particularly 16:21, seems to connote that Job meant someone else—that he was sure that in heaven he had a sponsor who could stand on his behalf and plead with God for his cause.[11]

Because his friends scoffed at him,[12] he poured out tears to God (16:20; cf. 16:16), longing that his heavenly witness as advocate would plead (argue his case) with God for a man,[13] that is, just as a man would do for his neighbor (16:21). Thus Job subtly chided his companions for failing to do what true friends ought to do, namely, plead his case. He needed an advocate because the time would soon be too late. His few years would soon come to an end (cf. 7:9-10; 10:21-22), and he could not possibly return (to appear in court) after death.

In a mournful tone, Job, cowering in despair from his yearning for an advocate, recognized that his spirit was exhausted, that his days were about gone, and that the grave was ready for him (17:1). And yet mockery surrounded him, and his eye, though tear filled, could only gaze on his companions' provocation. The word "provocation" is literally the plural "rebelliousnesses." Job could not easily forget the three men's words of

---

11. Many commentators, however, believe that Job was pleading with God that He be the advocate Himself.
12. The first half of 16:20 may be rendered, "my cries [or perhaps my inward thoughts] are my intercessors" (see Reichert, p. 85).
13. Job did not say, "O that a man might plead with God," but rather "O that he [i.e., my witness] would plead with God for a man [viz., for Job]."

accusation, which to him revealed an attitude of rebellion against himself and God. He was so overwhelmed with their persistent condemnatory words that he could only gaze in amazement.

d. *Job's disclaimer—of his friends* (17:3-5). Job then turned to God Himself, asking Him to lay down a pledge for Job (17:3a). This was apparently a custom in which a person, when going to trial, would give a bond or security to the other party as a certainty that no advantge would be taken of him. Changing the request to a question, Job asked, "Who is there that will be my guarantor?" (17:3b). Literally, he asked, "Who is there who will strike hands with me?" Striking hands was a practice of ratifying an agreement or business transaction (cf. Prov 6:1, see marg.; 11:15; 17:18, see marg.; 22:26, see marg.). Here Job was saying that no one would agree to stand up for him as his advocate at his trial. God, therefore, who is the Judge, must provide the bond and agree to appear in court.

This arrangement was necessary because God had kept the friends from understanding the truth about Job's innocence and would not exalt them (17:4). In fact, Job was so disgusted with them that he said they had turned against him in order selfishly to secure some of his property. Such a low crime would require that their children become blind (17:5).

e. *Job's despair—before his friends and in the face of death* (17:6-16). Like a roller coaster, Job's emotions moved up and down rapidly. After requesting God to provide a bond for him, he accused God of making him a byword (literally, proverb) before others. In other words, people had been talking about his sufferings in a derogatory way. Not only did they deride him with their words; they even spat on him—a terrible insult. What a picture of abject humiliation—a sick person, grieving over personal loss, chided by former friends, and then even rejected as a mangy, unwanted tramp by people who came to the garbage dump. So heavy was his grief that his "eye [had] also grown dim" (17:7a)[14] and his body had become emaciated through loss of weight ("all my members are as a shadow" [17:7b; cf. 16:8]).

Although his comforters of trouble mocked him (17:2) and people insulted him (17:6), Job saw his spirit suddenly rise; he

14. Eyes are referred to five times by Job (16:16, 20; 17:2, 5, 7).

became confident that the upright would be appalled at such malevolence shown to a righteous man and that the innocent would actively oppose godless (irreligious) people (17:8). Firm in his convictions, Job would "hold to his way" and in fact grow strong because he had clean hands; that is, he was innocent (17:9). He was so sure of his position that he challenged his trio of friends to renew their arguments, fully aware that they were totally lacking in wisdom (17:10).

Then he closed his second reply to Eliphaz in another dirge about death. He began this requiem with words expressing strong emotion, typical of a person who sees no point in living. Much of his life had passed, and many of his goals were unfulfilled (17:11).

In their first speeches, his friends had held out hope for Job, but to him it was like their trying to make night into day (17:12). Zophar, for example, had actually said that Job's darkness would become like morning (11:17). All Job had to look forward to, however, was death in Sheol; but there would be no hope there and certainly not any light. "If I look for Sheol as my home, I make my bed in the darkness" (17:13). He was so close to dying that he could call the pit (i.e., the grave) his father, and he could refer to the worm, which would consume his body, as his mother or sister (17:14). Any note of hope was so far removed from Job, now that he was about to die, that it would go down with him to Sheol and into the grave (17:15-16).

7

I Shall See God

3. *Bildad's second speech* (chap. 18)

Indignant at the indignity of Job's blatant words, Bildad lashed out impatiently. Bildad continued the theme Eliphaz had begun in this second round—the fate of the wicked. Bildad seemed to take his cues from his senior, for he touched on many of the same subjects, as the following reveals:

Darkness comes to the wicked	15:22-23, 30	18:5-6, 18
The wicked are like plants that do not thrive	15:30b, 32-33	18:16
Flames destroy the wicked	15:30, 34	18:15
The affluence of the wicked is removed	15:27-31	18:7, 15-16
Anguish terrifies the wicked	15:21, 24	18:11, 14
The tents of the wicked are destroyed	15:34	18:6, 14-15
The wicked oppose or do not know God	15:4, 13, 25-26	18:21

The lack of any extensive amount of fresh material in Bildad's speech is seen also in the fact that his notations about the wicked's being ensnared (18:8-10) were mentioned by Eliphaz in his first speech (5:13).

One the other hand, Eliphaz observed that the wicked man is destroyed by God (15:30c), whereas Bildad stressed that the wicked brings about his own downfall (18:7b-8). Eliphaz spoke of the guilty conscience that plagues the wicked with inner turmoil, but Bildad emphasized the external losses of the wicked— his material possessions (18:14-16), physical strength (18:7, 13), emotional security and serenity (18:8-11), fame (18:17-18), offspring (18:19).

It is interesting to observe that Bildad's second speech bears some similarities to his first speech. He began both speeches by asking "How long . . .?" (8:2; 18:2). He referred to Job's loss of his children (8:4; 18:19). He spoke of withering plants as a picture of the wicked's loss of his wealth (8:12-13, 16-19; 18:16). In each speech, Bildad mentioned the tent of the wicked (8:22; 18:15).

The second speech of Bildad's, like Eliphaz's second speech, is more caustic than his first. Whereas Bildad mentioned God by name six times in chapter 8, he referred to Him only once in chapter 18. Both men in their first speeches had held out hope for Job if he repented, but that hope was not considered a possibility by either man in his second speech.

In a number of his comments, Bildad was obviously responding to Job's words in chapter 16 and 17 or earlier chapters. Those replies will be mentioned in the following paragraphs.

a. *Bildad's denunciation of Job* (18:1-4). Bildad's impatience is obvious in his opening words: "How long will you hunt for words? Show understanding and then we can talk" (18:2). He likened Job's talk to unintelligent ramblings in which he was unsuccessfully trying to find the right words.[1] Bildad resented Job's calling him and his friends stupid beasts, as Job had implied (12:7-9). Job had said that God tore him in His anger (16:9); Bildad responded with a different idea—you tear yourself in *your* anger (18:4a). "Who does Job think he is," Bildad snapped, "that God would alter the course of nature just for *his* benefit?" (18:4b-c). Thus the friends' creed was again repeated: a man suffers in accord with his sins. Here too Bildad picked up a comment made earlier by Job (14:18) regarding rocks moving from their places.

b. *Bildad's description of the downfall of the wicked* (18:5-21). Bildad's ruthless account, obviously intended for Job, included the harassments of the ungodly person with material, physical, and emotional losses during his life, and no remembrance or posterity after death.

The light of the wicked, burning in his house and symbolizing

1. The words "hunt for" translate the Hebrew verb meaning "to lay snares," which occurs only here in the Old Testament.

continued prosperity, would go out, Bildad claimed (18:5-6; cf. Prov 13:9; 24:20). This was undoubtedly a retort to Job's assertion that "the tents of the destroyers prosper" (12:6), which in turn had been a rejoinder to Bildad's statement that "the tent of the wicked will be no more" (8:22). The ungodly man, though self-confident in his "vigorous stride," would be weakened by the schemes he had planned against others (18:7).

Six words for "trap" are used in 18:8-10; in this passage, more synonyms are used for this word than are used for "trap" in any other Old Testament passage. The "net" is used for catching birds (cf. Prov 1:17) or men, and the "webbing" is a light, interwoven covering over a pit (18:8). The "snare" is a bird trap, and the "trap" that "snaps shut" is one with some kind of mesh (18:9). The "noose" hidden in the ground is a rope with a noose, and the "trap" on the path is a general term (18:10). Bildad heaped together those synonyms to stress many imminent dangers facing the wicked person and resulting in his being continually frightened and harried (18:11) as he turned from one direction to another, trying unsuccessfully to avoid dangers.

"His strength is famished" (18:12) should read "his calamity is hungry," meaning that the troubles he faced were about to seize him. "His skin is devoured by disease" (18:13a) is a heartless allusion to Job's skin problem. "The first-born of death" (which "devours his limbs") may mean "death in its most terrible form."[2] A better meaning may be that among man's diseases—known as death's children because they serve death's purposes—Job's was the worst.

Bildad continued by saying that Job would be torn from the security of his tent and dragged like a captive "before the king of terrors" (18:14), death being personified as a king bringing about fear. Although Job "sought to flee from terrors, he is brought at last to the king of them."[3]

Having spoken of disease, which leads to death (18:13), and of death itself (18:14), Bildad then elaborated on the results of death (18:15-21). Nothing of his own family or possessions will

2. H. H. Rowley, *Job*, p. 162.
3. A. B. Davidson, *The Book of Job*, p. 135.

be in his tent, and brimstone (sulphur) will be "scattered on his habitation" (18:15). The brimstone may refer to God's sending fire in judgment (Gen 19:24; Deut 29:22-23), to the use of sulphur to fumigate a room where a corpse had lain, or to Job's own catastrophe whereby his sheep were burned (1:16).

In the words "his roots are dried below" (18:16) Bildad may have subtly referred to Job's words (14:8). The wicked man, Bildad said, would become so devastated that he would be like a rootless, branchless tree. No one would remember him (18:17), and he would be banished into darkness, that is, into death or solitude (18:18). No offspring or posterity would survive the wicked man (18:19). Lack of descendants was considered a terrible fate, for a man's name would not be perpetuated. So calamitous would be the fate of the wicked (18:20) that people everywhere, in the west and east, would be appalled.

The unusual word translated "wicked" (18:21) means "a deviate person." For Bildad there was no mistaking the wicked man's destiny—nor the person whom Bildad had in mind. Because Job had lost his possessions, children, wealth, and reputation, and had been ensnared by numerous calamities, he was a deviate and one "who does not know God." Pronounced with a note of finality, Bildad's summary capsuled the old tune: wickedness results in suffering.

4. Job's second reply to Bildad (chap. 19)

Job responded to Bildad's speech in ways similar to his reply to Eliphaz. In chapters 16 and 17 and then in chapter 19, Job arraigned the uselessness of their wordy assaults, accused God of attacking him as an enemy, and exhibited a sudden shaft of hope that acquittal would be forthcoming. Chapter 19, however, includes two elements not found in chapters 16 and 17: Job's sense of being forsaken by relatives, friends, and servants; and his profound assurance that his Redeemer lives, and that he will see God. This chapter is a skyscraper among the forty-two chapters of Job that form the beautiful skyline of this poetic masterpiece. After decrying hostility from his accusers (19:1-6), from God (19:7-12), and from his relatives and friends (19:13-22), the suffering saint rose from the depths of his broken spirit to the heights of renewed confidence in his God (19:23-29).

a. *Hostility from his accusers* (19:1-6). Twice Bildad began his speeches with "How long?" (8:2; 18:2). Now Job threw the question back at him by asking the trio, "How long will you torment me, and crush me with words?" (19:2). Rather than helping, their bitter words had only added to his vexation, causing him to feel pulverized under the emotional weight. They repeatedly insulted him ("ten times" is an idiom meaning "often") and were not ashamed to wrong him (19:3). Even if he had sinned—he did not admit that he had erred; he merely said "if"— that was his own business and was not their concern (19:4). Their tactics were clear to Job: they were acting superior to him (cf. 12:3; 13:2) and arguing that his afflictions were proof of God's displeasure. But he had news for them. They needed to know that it was *God* who had wronged him (19:5-6). The word "wronged" could be translated "perverted," the same word used by Bildad when he asked "Does God pervert justice?" (8:3). Here Job declared outright that God had indeed perverted justice in his case. Bildad was all wrong in intimating that Job was being trapped by his own nets (18:8-10); it was *God* who had "closed His net around" Job (19:6*b*). This word for "net" differs from the six words for nets and traps earlier used (18:8-10). "This is the hunter's net, into which he drives animals."[4]

b. *Hostility from God* (19:7-12). In both responses to Eliphaz (6:4; 7:20; and 16:12-14), Job had said that God was treating him like an enemy. In his second answer to Bildad, he again reverted to that view. His statement about God's having perverted his cause (19:6) led him from the hostility of his friends to hostility at the hands of God. It is noteworthy that both he and his colleagues regarded Job's misfortunes as coming from God's hand, but their reasons differed vastly. The three friends looked on the misfortunes as retribution for sin, whereas Job saw them as totally unfair actions.

This injustice from God was compounded by His ignoring Job's shouts of "violence" and his cries for help (19:7). Then

4. Rowley, p. 167.

God's hostile, violent actions were enumerated—ten in all (19: 8-12). To feel the impact of Job's words, one should emphasize the word "He" as one reads these verses. Job was attributing his afflictions directly to God.

God had restricted Job's travel by placing obstructions in his path (cf. 3:23, where Job voiced a similar complaint); He had darkened his paths so that he could only grope along (19:8). God had stripped his hands from him and removed the crown from his head, a way of referring to his loss of esteem as a leading citizen (19:9). God also was breaking him down on every side, as if He were demolishing a building, so that Job was almost dead, and He had uprooted his hope like a tree (19:10; cf. 14: 7). Changing the metaphor to warfare (19:11-12), Job said that God was angry with him (cf. 16:9), treating him like an enemy (cf. 13:24). In military fashion, God had treated Job like a beleaguered city, surrounding him with troops who built a rampart against the city wall to besiege it. When Job added that the troops camped around his tent, he expressed the extreme unfairness of God's actions. Why would numerous troops need to surround one meager man in a mere tent?

Some of these words about God's belligerent operations seem to be in direct response to Bildad's earlier remarks (chap. 18). Bildad had cited the troubles of the wicked, and Job carried them back to their source—God Himself.[5]

Carter suggests that Job was not ascribing these notions of enmity to God, but to the friends' traditional view of God. He argues that Job's words would otherwise be blasphemous.[6] To Carter, Job was simply following the implications of their view: If Job were suffering for his sins, then God was an enemy. This, however, seems to be reading into the text. Nowhere did Job say or imply, "If your view is correct, then God is my enemy." Instead Job came out directly with the conviction, "God *is* my enemy." Job was frustrated with more than their view of God; he was frustrated with God Himself, whose actions appeared to

5. Cf. 19:8*b* with 18:5-6, 18 (darkness present); 19:9 with 18:16-17 (honor removed); 19:10*a* with 18:7, 12 (brought down); 19:10*b* with 18:16 (tree uprooted); 19:12 with 18:14 (insecure in his tent).
6. Charles W. Carter, "The Book of Job," in *The Wesleyan Bible Commentary,* ed. Charles W. Carter, vol. 2 (Grand Rapids: Eerdmans, 1968), p. 104.

be grossly unjust. Job's opinion did not amount to blasphemy;[7] instead, it revealed an honest assessment of the facts as he saw them.

c. *Hostility from relatives, friends, and servants* (19:13-22). Job bemoaned his loneliness, another aspect of his suffering. He had been bereft of comrades,[8] acquaintances, relatives, close friends, house servants, his own private slave, his wife, brothers, and even young children (19:13-18). These groups move from the outer circle of social acquaintances to the most intimate relationships, and from persons on a level with Job to those who were inferior to him.

It was painful enough to be rejected by friends, but even worse was the rejection by "those who live in [his] house" (i.e., overnight guests of household servants) and his maids (19:15). It was "bitter humiliation"[9] to be ignored by his personal attendant when he called him and even begged him (19:16). His breath was offensive to his wife, probably meaning that she detested his intimate embraces because of disease-caused halitosis. He was even despised by his "own brothers" (literally, sons of my womb, meaning either his sons, who were the offspring of his wife's womb, or his brothers, who were offspring of his mother's womb.[10] Job had said that God handed him over to urchins (16:11); now he added that those young children despised him (19:18). Their contempt is especially deplorable, for children were to pay great respect to adults. Even when Job stood up (to gain their respect?), they spoke against him. All his "associates" (literally, males of my council, meaning close friends) abhorred him; probably included were Eliphaz, Bildad, and Zophar. And those he loved turned against him (19:19).

Job felt ostracized not only by those in his outer circle of ac-

---

7. Blasphemy is a settled attitude of antagonistic animosity toward God, revealed by a railing defamation of character. Job voiced frustration, exasperation, and disgust at God's apparent injustice, but he did not voice a belligerent rejection of God.
8. The word "brothers" may mean literally his blood relatives, or figuratively his comrades or cohorts who were of the same social strata in life. Perhaps the latter is intended.
9. Victor E. Reichert, *Job*, p. 97.
10. Probably his brothers are intended; cf. 3:10, where "my . . . womb" means "my mother's womb," as the NASB has it.

quaintances, but even by those loved ones who would normally be expected to stand by a suffering relative. Added to all this emotional anguish was his physical pain: "My bone clings to my skin and my flesh" (19:20a); that is, he had lost weight and was emaciated to skin and bones (cf. 16:8; 18:13). Job's next words, "I have escaped only by the skin of my teeth" (19:20b), have become a cliché meaning "I barely escaped, keeping nothing but my life," or, "I had a close call." However, another possible meaning is that "the skin of my teeth" means Job's gums. In that case, the thought would be that his body was so totally dissipated by disease that even his teeth had fallen out and only his gums were unaffected.

In a sorrowful whine of misery, Job repeated his plea that they pity him (literally, deal graciously). Surprisingly, he addressed them, "O you my friends," perhaps in sarcasm, for they had certainly not acted like true friends. He turned to them because "the hand of God [had] struck" him (19:21). God had persecuted him, so why should they do the same? Why were they "not satisfied with [his] flesh?"; that is, why should they continue to malign him (to eat another's flesh was to curse him). One can sense the pitiful frustration of a defeated man turning for help first from God to man; and then when man fails him, "in a burst of sublime confidence he returns from man to God."[11]

d. *Certainty of seeing God* (19:23-29). Job was at his lowest point. Friends and family had all deserted him. Human help had vanished. He was alone in his misery with not even one person to console him, to lend support by saying "I understand." His body was racked with pain, and he was the brutal object of God's unfair torments.

"But it is just here, when everything is blackest, that his faith . . . like the rainbow in the cloud . . . shines with a marvelous splendour."[12]

Job 19:23-27 is probably the best known portion of the book. It is a grand climax, the peak of Job's confidence in a future vindication of his cause. It is a "magnificent burst of faith."[13]

11. A. S. Peake, cited by Rowley, p. 171.
12. W. B. MacLeod, *The Afflictions of the Righteous* (London: Hodder & Stoughton, n.d.), p. 172.
13. Ibid., p. 173.

Job began this outcry of faith by requesting that his words of protestation be given permanence by being "written" and "inscribed in a book," no doubt a scroll (19:23). Then he requested another form of writing: that with an "iron stylus" (i.e., an engraving tool) and with lead his words would be "engraved in the rock forever" (19:24). The lead was not the material written on, but was probably melted and poured into the grooves inscribed in the rock. This memorial would allow future generations to judge the justice of his case.

Verses 25 and 26 have been variously interpreted because of a number of uncertainties in the text. The first problem pertains to the identity of the Redeemer. Some scholars say that he is a person other than God because of Job's similar requests for an arbiter between himself and God (9:33) and for a witness or advocate (16:19) and because Job still sensed God's distance later (23:3). Others identify the Redeemer as God Himself because of the parallel statement, "I shall see God" (19:26) and because his witness was said to be "in heaven" and "on high" (16:19).

"Redeemer," used forty-four times in the Old Testament, comes from a verb meaning "to lay claim to a person or thing, to free or deliver." A redeemer in the Old Testament was a person who provided protection or legal preservation for a close relative who could not do so for himself. He could redeem the relative's property that had passed into other hands (cf. Lev 25: 23-25; Ruth 4:4-15); he could avenge a slain relative (Num 35: 19-27; 2 Sam 14:11; 1 Kings 16:11); he could marry his brother's childless widow (Ruth 4:10); he could buy a close relative out of slavery (Lev 25:47-55); and he could defend his cause in a lawsuit (Psalm 119:154; Prov 23:11; Jer 50:34).

Verse 25 stresses the word "I": "I, even I, know that my Redeemer lives." Although Job expected death, he knew that his Defender, or Protector, was alive and would certainly take up his cause and vindicate him. Then Job added, "And at the last He will take His stand on the earth" (19:25b). The words "at the last" have been taken by some scholars to mean in the future or at the last minute. But because the Hebrew word is an adjective, not an adverb, it describes the Redeemer, the One who will

89

rise, and therefore the word should be rendered "the last One," or "He who comes last or later." God will have the final say, as it were.

What does "stand on the earth" mean? The word translated "earth" is literally "dust," and some scholars understand it to mean the grave, as dust is so used (7:21; 17:16; 20:11; 21:26; 34:15). However, "dust" also can mean the earth (5:6; 8:19; 14:8; 41:33, marg.). The latter may be preferred. Job's thought is that his living Vindicator, who will be the last One and thus will have the final word, will stand on the earth as a witness stands in a trial and will testify to Job's innocence for all to hear.

"Even after my skin is destroyed" (19:26a) is the most difficult portion of this passage to interpret. According to some scholars the verb should be rendered "destroyed," as the NASB does.[14] Other scholars suggest that the verb means "surround" and that the clause should be rendered "afterward with my skin they surround this [namely, my body]."[15] The translation "flayed" is a third possibility, preferred by this writer. Job was not expecting to be flayed alive, but rather was referring figuratively to the peeling of his skin as a picture of death encroaching upon him slowly. The verb means "stripped off" and is used in Isaiah (10:34) of cutting off branches of a tree. In the Hebrew, the word "this" appears at the end of the line and is not translated in the NASB and other versions. It may refer back to skin, "this skin of mine," or, perhaps more likely, it may mean "thus": "after my skin is stripped off thus [in this way]."

The King James Version supplies the words "worms" and "body" ("though after my skin worms destroy this body") in an effort to supply a noun for the verb "destroy," which is plural, and to supply an object to the word "this." However, the plural verb in Hebrew without a subject may be rendered as a passive and need not have a subject. It can therefore legitimately be rendered "is stripped off" (rather than "worms destroy").

14. A. Guillaume assumes this view and supports it by explaining that the "Arabs sometimes use the word 'skin' when they are speaking of a man's body" ("The Unity of the Book of Job," *The Annual of the Leeds University Oriental Society* 4 [1963-1965]: 44).
15. This view is supported by Rudolph E. Honsey, "Exegetical Paper on Job 19:23-27," *Wisconsin Lutheran Quarterly* 67 (1970): 172-84.

The second half of verse 26 is also subject to interpretation. When Job said, "from my flesh I shall see God," did he mean from the vantage point of his flesh (i.e., in his flesh while still alive) or did he mean, apart from his flesh (i.e., after death)? The former view is supported by Job's statement in the next verse that his eyes would see God. However, the poetic feature known as parallelism suggests that the two lines of 19:26 be taken together. Because death is implied in 19:26*a,* it is to be expected in 19:26*b.* Furthermore, Job did expect to die soon (16:18-22; 17:1, 16; 30:23). Also, the word "from" normally means "apart from."

Job was so certain that he would see God that he repeated the thought: "whom I myself shall behold" (19:27). "See" (19:26) and "behold" (19:27) are the same Hebrew word, meaning to see in a vision or in a supernatural condition. His gazing on God, his Redeemer, for all eternity would certainly be for his benefit (for "myself"). Then Job added, apparently for emphasis, "and whom my eyes shall see and not another." He himself would see God, face to face, and he would not be a stranger or enemy to God, as he was then.

Such an amazing thought, however, so overwhelmed Job that he exclaimed, "my heart faints within me" (19:27*c*). His heart (literally, kidneys, considered by the Hebrews to be the seat of deepest emotions) was spent or consumed within him (literally, in his bosom). He was exhausted emotionally by the astounding prospect of a face-to-face encounter with God.

When did Job expect to be vindicated by his living Redeemer? At least three answers are given: (1) during his lifetime (then why did he desire that his words be engraved for future generations, and how can this view be reconciled with his words "after my skin is destroyed"?), (2) after death and in a bodily resurrected state (but though he spoke of seeing God with his eyes, he said his seeing would be apart from his flesh), (3) in the afterlife, but not in a resurrected body. The latter seems to be as far as Job went, because he did not give a definitive statement about the resurrection. He said "[apart] from my flesh," not "with new resurrected flesh." Also, the resurrection view does not reckon with the then current belief in Sheol (7:9, 21; 10:21-22;

91

14:7-14; 16:22). He longed to see God—and knew that he would because his living Redeemer-Vindicator would stand on his behalf and plead his case. This was the longed-for Arbiter (9:33), Witness-Advocate (16:19), whom we know as Jesus Christ, the Son of God. Job's assurance of vindication after death was a giant step in his walk of faith and another indication that he was sure the three friends were wrong in their accusations. Death, inevitable and imminent, would be a gate, not a wall, to solving his problem.

Job then turned to his companions in the two closing verses of his speech: "If you say, 'How shall we persecute him? [to try to get him to accept our view]' and 'the root of the matter is found in him'[16] then be afraid of the sword for yourselves." Then Job stated the reason for this warning: "for wrath brings the punishment of the sword, so that you may know there is judgment." Job was saying that God's wrath on their sinful ways against him would result in their deaths by the sword, and they would thus experience the judgment God brings on the wicked—which judgment they had been saying he would feel. Again, Job was certain that he was right and that they were wrong. It was this confidence that enabled him to look beyond this life to vindication by God and fellowship with God.

16. Translation suggested by Reichert (p. 101), and Rowley (p. 175), and others.

8

Why Do the Wicked Live?

5. *Zophar's second speech* (chap. 20)

Impatient and angry, Zophar blasted out at Job in a stinging
diatribe. His words were as venomous as the cobras and vipers
he mentioned (20:14, 16). Whereas Eliphaz in his second
speech had spoken of the distress of the wicked man and Bildad
had said the wicked man is trapped, Zophar stressed that the
wicked loses his wealth. Zophar's words in this chapter are the
most stinging of the three comrades' speeches so far.

a. *The aroused anger of Zophar* (20:1-3). Zophar began with
the word "therefore," perhaps meaning "because of what Job had
just said." Zophar, however, did not make any reply to Job's
burst of confidence about his Redeemer. His "disquieting
thoughts" (not calm reflections, but thoughts that disturb) and
his "inward agitation" prompted him to speak again (20:2).
Job had told the three friends that they had insulted him numerous times (19:3), but now Zophar retorted disgustedly that
Job insulted *him*. Irascible Zophar, hinting that he was superior,
told Job, "the spirit of my understanding makes me answer" (20:
3). This may have been in response to Job's earlier question,
"What plagues you that you answer?" (16:3).

b. *The brief prosperity of the wicked man* (20:4-11). Because Job knows so much, Zophar implied, does he not know
what has always been true from the time of the first man—that
the triumphing (celebrations) of the wicked is short and the joy
of the godless (irreverent) is momentary (20:4-5)? It is an
eternal principle that everyone knows. Bildad had said that the
godless will perish (8:13-19), and Eliphaz had said that the
wicked man will have emptiness before his time (15:29-35).
Zophar's entire second speech is an angry elaboration of Eliphaz's
words, "nor will his wealth endure" (15:29).

Zophar said that a man's high position may mount up to the heavens and his head may touch the clouds—in success and influence—but he would perish forever, like dung, and people who knew him would not know where he was. What a striking contrast: high as the heavens, low as dung; prominent in leadership, presence unknown. Such a man would fly away like a dream, be gone and forgotten, and no one would be able to find him. Like Bildad, Zophar said that the eminent but wicked person would be chased away (18:18; 20:8b). He would be unseen, whereas before he had been looked on with respect and awe, and even the place where he lived would no longer see him (20:9). His family would be affected too; his loss of wealth would result in his sons' being "reduced to the humiliating condition of asking the aid of the most needy and abject."[1] They would be beggars of beggars.

Even more humiliating, his hands (meaning the father himself or his sons) would be obligated to return wealth that he acquired dishonestly (20:10). This is one of the chapter's few references to the sins of the wicked man; most of the chapter dwells on his losses.[2]

Although the wicked man may have possessed youthful vigor, Zophar said, it would die with him (20:11).

Prominent, wealthy, energetic—that was Zophar's portrait of the wicked. Worthless like dung, fleeting like a dream, absent, poor, perishing in the dust—such would soon be the lot of the wicked, and obviously of Job. Those piercing words no doubt hurt Job deeply.

c. *The certain punishment of sin* (20:12-19). A man may seek to enjoy sin, retaining it as long as possible—like something sweet in his mouth—and he may desire it (literally, have compassion on it) and not want to let go of it, but Zophar said that it would become poisonous to him. It would be like food turning bad in his stomach, becoming like the venom of cobras with-

1. Albert Barnes, *Notes, Critical, Illustrative, and Practical, on the Book of Job*, 1:338.
2. The sins are unethically acquired wealth (20:10, 19), enjoyment of evil (20:12), hiding of evil (20:12), heartless accumulation of wealth (20:15, 22, 23), oppression of the poor (20:19), stealing (20:19), devouring of others' wealth to the point of having nothing else to acquire (20:20).

in him (20:12-14). "Venom" is literally "gall," for "the ancients believed that serpents secreted poison in the gall bladder."[3] Sin may be pleasant when committed, but its consequences are bitter.

Zophar then continued the subject of eating, but changed it from the swallowing of sin to the swallowing of riches (20:15). He said that such a greedy person is not allowed to retain his ill-got wealth. God causes him to vomit it up. This illustration is a coarser way of repeating what Zophar had said earlier: "His hands give back his wealth" (20:10). Furthermore, Zophar added, the wicked man's acquisition of wealth is like his sucking in the poison of cobras; it soon destroys him, as an infectious poison would. And the viper's tongue (fangs) kill him (20:16).

"He does not [or, shall not] look at the streams, the rivers flowing with honey and curds" (20:17). Rivers flowing with honey and curdled milk (a delicacy in the Middle East) were symbols of prosperity and ease. Zophar said that even what the wicked man worked for must be given up without being used (cf. 20:15), and riches acquired by trading cannot be enjoyed (20:18). The reason for this loss is that he sinned by oppressing the poor and abandoning them to their fate. He even seized the houses of the poor (20:19).

d. *The quick anger of God toward the wealthy wicked* (20:20-29). Because of his insatiable greed ("he knew no quiet in his belly" [20:20, marg.]), said Zophar, the wealthy man cannot retain (or resist) anything he desires. Just as nothing was left that he had not devoured, so nothing he had acquired would be left (20:21). At the peak of his luxury, he would be in distress; and those whom he reduced to misery would turn against him (20:22). When he had filled his belly (this and the previous reference to belly [20:20, marg.] both spoke of greed), God's anger would be cast on him, and He would rain it on him into his intestines (20:23).[4] An interesting contrast is presented here by Zophar: the wicked fills his belly with wealth, but God rains His anger into his bowels.

In addition, Zophar said that God would attack the wicked man as with an army, so his death was inevitable. He may escape

3. H. H. Rowley, *Job*, p. 179.
4. "Inner flesh" is meant here, not "while he is eating" as the NASB has it.

95

an iron weapon (a sword or spear) but be killed by a bronze arrow (literally, bow, representing by metonymy an arrow). The wounded person would try to save himself by pulling out of his body the arrow, which has pierced even his gall, and terrors would overwhelm him (20:24-25). Zophar painted a ghastly picture of the end of a man who is the object of God's wrath. Zophar may very likely have been enlarging on what Job had previously said: "His arrows surround me. Without mercy He splits my kidneys open; He pours out my gall on the ground" (16:13).

Following the wicked man's death, utter darkness would overtake his treasures, and fire would consume him (probably meaning his possessions) and the survivors in his tent (his wife and children) (20:26). This reference to darkness and fire consuming his possessions and tent was a cruel reminder of Job's calamities (chap. 1).

Job had stated that his Witness and Advocate were in heaven, ready to defend him, and he had appealed to the earth to allow his need for vindication to remain visible (16:18-19). However, Zophar denied the possibility of either. Instead, the heavens would "reveal his iniquity" and "the earth [would] rise up against him" (20:27) in condemnation, not vindication.

His possessions would be carried away[5] and washed away, evidence of God's anger (20:28). Then, in one final blow, Zophar summarized his arraignment with the brutal words, "This is the wicked man's portion from God, even the heritage decreed[6] to him by God" (20:29). In this compassionless peroration, Zophar sought to leave Job with no escape from the inevitable conclusion that he was the wicked man of whom Zophar had been speaking and that Job's experience could not possibly be an exception to the universal law of divine administration of judgment on sin. In this invective attack, Zophar had spoken a number of truths—for example, God judges sin—but he was wrong in asserting that the wicked man's prosperity is *always* evanescent, and he was wrong in applying this assertion to Job. Thus

5. "Deport" is literally "be carried away into captivity."
6. "Decreed" is literally "of his word," meaning "in accord with his stated purpose."

Zophar's clobbering ended on a firm note, similar to the conclusions of Eliphaz's first speech (5:27) and Bildad's second speech (18:21).

6. *Job's second reply to Zophar* (chap. 21)

In the first cycle of speeches, the friends argued that God consistently blesses the good and punishes the wicked. Job, however, did not speak to that point specifically until all three had spoken. The same is true of Job in the second cycle. He waited until they had all voiced themselves on the subject of the testing of the wicked before he responded to their claim. After Eliphaz spoke the second time, Job elaborated on God's role as his enemy. And after Bildad's second address, Job again elaborated on God's role as his enemy. But in chapter 21, Job countered the view of the three about the destruction of the wicked. And because Zophar's words were even more virulent than the others, Job replied more directly to him.

a. *Job's call for silence* (21:1-6). As the sufferer began his bold reply, he requested that the three counselors "listen carefully," for it was only then that they would be offering him consolation (21:2).[7] Their silence would be more comforting than their words (and more wise [cf. 13:5]). Sarcastically he added that if they would do him that favor, then after he finished, they could continue their mocking. Job said that he was not complaining to man, so why should they become exercised over his words. He was actually complaining to God, and because He was silent, Job had reason to be impatient (21:3-4). Just a look at him ought to have astounded them into silence—yet they had gazed at him and kept gabbing. Job himself was certainly horrified when he looked at himself (21:5-6).

b. *Job's claim that wicked men live in prosperity* (21:7-16). Job immediately opposed the view propounded in the second round. If his counselors were correct, "why do the wicked still live, continue on, also become very powerful?" (21:7). How could this incontrovertible fact square with their contention? This verse includes the first of several specific contrasts between what Job and Zophar each said:

7. "Consolation" is the same word Eliphaz had used earlier (15:11).

Zophar (chap. 20)	*Job* (chap. 21)
The wicked . . .	The wicked . . .
perish like dung (v. 7)	live (v. 7)
triumph only a short time (v. 5)	continue on (v. 7)
lose their loftiness and youthful vigor (vv. 6, 11)	become very powerful (v. 7)
lose the survivors in their tent (v. 26)	enjoy their children and grandchildren (v. 8)
lose the wealth in their houses (vv. 21, 23, 28)	live safely in their houses (v. 9a) and their herds increase (v. 10)
suffer God's fierce anger (vv. 23, 28)	know nothing of God's rod of judgment (v. 9)
have sons who must beg from the poor (v. 10)	have happy children (vv. 11-12)
will have their riches expelled out of their bellies (v. 15) and cannot enjoy prosperity and ease (vv. 17-18)	spend their days in prosperity (v. 13)
have their sins revealed (v. 27)	get away with sinful defiance of God (vv. 14-15)
do not suffer for their own sins (v. 10; 21:19)	suffer for their own sins (vv. 19-21)
are forgotten at death (vv. 7-9).	are given an honorable burial (vv. 32-33).

In these stark contrasts, Job categorically counteracted every dogmatic assertion of Zophar.

According to Job, Zophar had let his preconceived theological system blind him to the facts. The picture Job painted of wicked people included those living to old age, those who were prominent, those who had their children and grandchildren happy and around them, those who lived in security, those who owned fertile herds (a sign of divine blessing), those who enjoyed merriment[8] and peace, those who were wealthy, and those who were dying peacefully. In addition, the wicked, Job observed, saw no need for serving God; they were doing well by themselves. Therefore, they deliberately rejected Him, not wanting to know Him. They would gain nothing from Him beyond what they already had (21:14-15).[9]

Job's assessment, "Behold, their prosperity is not in their hands" (21:16a), may mean that their prosperity comes not from themselves but from God. Job then rejected such principles (21:16b); but his presenting the wicked in such glowing terms did not mean he sided with them or desired to follow their plans.

c. *Job's claim that the wicked, whether prosperous or poor, die for their own sins* (21:17-26). To Bildad's contention that "the light of the wicked goes out" (18:5) and "calamity is ready at his side" (18:12), Job objected: "How often is the lamp of the wicked put out, or [how often] does their calamity fall on them?" (21:17). And Job also contradicted Zophar's view that God deals out anger on the wicked at the height of his luxurious enjoyment of sin (20:23) by asking, "Does God apportion destruction in His anger?" (21:17c). And again by a question (21:18), Job added that the wicked are not destroyed suddenly like straw blown by the wind or like chaff blown by the storm (a refutation of Zophar's words [20:8-9]?). Job anticipated that his companions might seek to answer his arguments by suggesting that the sin of the wicked will be judged on his children. Job objected to that attempted way out by stating that a dead man would not know what his children were suffering nor would he care, and that the wicked man ought to suffer retribution for his own sins, drinking God's wrath himself (21:19-21).

By still another question (21:22), Job pointed out that the three friends were presuming by their generalizations to tell God what to do. "You have no right or ability to teach God anything.

8. The musical instruments mentioned (21:12)—timbrel, harp, flute—are a percussion instrument, a stringed instrument, and a wind instrument.
9. This cleverly refuted Bildad's claim that the one "who does not know God" (18:21) suffers; here Job showed that the one who rejects God does *not* suffer.

He is not bound by your limited theology. After all, He is the Judge of those in heaven[10] and thus of every human being."

Instead of all wicked men dying suddenly at the height of their prosperity, Job observed that this fate holds true for only some of the wicked. Some die while they are strong, peaceful, satisfied ("his sides are filled out with fat" [cf. Psalm 73:4]), and healthy ("the marrow of his bones is moist"), while others die in bitterness, having experienced no blessings in life at all (21:23-25). Death is the great leveler, for though vastly different in life, both men are together in the dust, and in the grave the bodies of both are covered with worms (21:26). In these verses (21:23-26) Job was not arguing that the wicked always prosper and the good are always unfortunate, but that one's character cannot be determined by his lot in life. Job's opponents should not seek to tell God to judge a person's life by his bank account or his medical chart. All men die, and only God can be the accurate Judge of their lives, regardless of the presence or absence of wealth or health.

d. *Job's claim that the wicked die in prosperity* (21:27-34). Job quipped that he knew their line of argument, their plans for destroying his reputation (21:27). By asking "where is the tent . . . of the wicked?" (21:28), the counselors had insinuated that Job was sinful. Job was quoting Bildad (8:22; 18:21) and possibly Zophar (20:28). All they needed to do to see who was right was to ask travelers, those who had seen other parts of the world (21:29). Travelers would confirm Job's viewpoint that "the wicked is reserved for [spared from] the day of calamity; they will be led forth [delivered for execution] at the day of fury" (21:30).[11]

The wicked person is allowed, Job contended, to continue on in his evil ways, without anyone's daring to confront him or to requite him (21:31). He is honored, not only in life, but even after life, for people guard his tomb and crowd his casket in the funeral procession; and these evidences indicate his popularity.

---

10. Or, "He judges from on high," that is, He adjudicates the universe from His position in heaven.
11. Some scholars, however, take this verse as a quotation, introduced by the words "You say."

What is more, even the clods of dirt where he will be buried will be sweet to him (21:32-33).

In view of these observations, the only evaluation Job could make of the three friends was that their comfort was vain (empty) and their answers faithless (21:34, marg.). Job concluded the second round by announcing that in spite of all their talk they had been no help whatsoever.

9

God, Where Are You?

D. THE THIRD CYCLE OF SPEECHES (chaps. 22—37)

In cycle one, Job's visitors implied that Job was a sinner and appealed to him to repent. In cycle two, they insinuated that he was guilty and stressed the terrible fate of the wicked, but gave no opportunity for repentance. In the third cycle, they attacked with open accusations of specific sins, and only Eliphaz again gave a call for Job to turn back to God. Job stood his ground in response to all three rounds of attack. He denied the premise of their implications, he denied their assertion that the wicked always suffer, and he denied that he himself was a deliberate transgressor.

1. *Eliphaz's third speech* (chap. 22)

In Eliphaz's first foray, he had displayed a modicum of courtesy; in his second onslaught, politeness was absent; in his third assault, he was openly discourteous. He did not even mention Job's wordiness; he just tore into Job abruptly.

a. *Eliphaz asserted God's disinterest in Job* (22:1-5). Eliphaz argued that God does not need man. Neither the "vigorous man" (literally, strong man) nor even the wise man, who is more honored than the physically eminent, can be of any use to Him[1] (22: 2). God receives no pleasure from man's righteousness or any profit from man's integrity (22:3). Obviously to Eliphaz, God was not requiting Job for being reverent; therefore, the only explanation of God's actions was that He was punishing Job for his great wickedness (22:4-5). God, concerned only with justice, needed to meet with man only when retribution was required by man's sin. If Job were righteous, Eliphaz asserted, God would

1. The last word of 22:2 should be "Him" (i.e., God), not "himself."

not need to respond, giving Job blessings in return. Job's uprightness could not please or benefit God. It was only because Job had sinned that God's alarm system went off, causing Him to penalize Job.

Eliphaz's brand of theology was an attempt to explain God's silence, but it mixed error with truth. In one sense God does not need man, yet He longs for man's companionship, worship, and love. God does judge iniquity, but that is not His only occasion for communication with man.

b. *Eliphaz accused Job of social deviations* (22:6-11). Without any evidence whatsoever, Eliphaz openly charged Job with several social evils, which elaborated his general indictment already stated (22:5). Eliphaz fabricated a catalog of crimes typical of a man in a position of power and affluence.

1. According to Eliphaz, Job had taken pledges from his brothers (i.e., countrymen, the same word as in 19:13a) without cause and stripped men naked (22:6). Old Testament law required that if a man was forced to give his outer garment to a creditor as a pledge of payment, the garment was to be returned to him at night so that he would have its protection from the cold (Exod 22:26-27; Deut 24:10-13). To keep a garment-pledge was an inexcusable sin, for it meant leaving the debtor practically naked and thus helpless. The irony of this falsification is that Job, being wealthy, would have had no reason for such a misdemeanor. Eliphaz was thus seeking to demonstrate the debased condition of Job's morality. Job, however, answered this charge (31:19-22).

2. Eliphaz accused Job of refusing to give water to the weary and bread to the hungry (22:7). This indictment pointed to hardness of heart, to lack of customary concern for the needy. Again, affluent Job certainly could have afforded to give water to thirsty, tired travelers and an occasional meal to hungry overnight guests. Job answered this charge also (31:17-22).

3. A third malefaction Eliphaz thrust at Job was his abuse of widows and orphans (22:9). (Verse 8 reads, "But the earth belongs to the mighty man, and the honorable man dwells in it." Interpreters vary in their understanding of this verse. Some critics unjustifiably seek to eliminate the verse entirely; others want to place it after 22:14; and still others preface the verse with the

words "For you believe," and put the verse in quotation marks so that Eliphaz was saying that the reason for Job's unhospitable actions toward travelers was his arrogance in thinking he owned the earth.[2] Other interpreters see Job's arrogance as a statement by Eliphaz, not a quotation from Job. Still others take it as a charge separate from the one in 22:9: Job aggressively seized real estate owned by others. Regardless of how the verse is to be understood, the intended arraignment is clear: Job was the "mighty man" and the "honorable man"[3] with extensive property holdings.)

To reject widows and crush orphans was an atrocious felony, because widows and their children (orphans were usually father-less children living with their mothers) were subject to social and economic abuses, being without male protection and leadership. This sin was condemned (Exod 22:22; Deut 27:19; Jer 7:6; 22: 3; Zech 7:10), and Job repudiated the accusation (31:16-22).

The resultant reprisal for such sins was snares, dread, darkness, flood (22:10-11). Three of these thoughts were picked up by Eliphaz from Bildad's second speech: (*a*) the "snare" is the bird trap Bildad had mentioned (18:9*a*); (*b*) "sudden dread terri-fies" calls to mind "all around terrors frighten him" (18:11); and (*c*) the "darkness" would underscore "he is driven from light into darkness" (18:18*a*). These words would again be painful reminders of Job's catastrophic losses and emotional paroxysms.

c. *Eliphaz accused Job of spiritual defiance* (22:12-20). Be-hind these social inequities was an attitude of insolence against the Sovereign, Eliphaz averred. God is in "the height of heaven," certainly higher than the almost infinite distance of the stars (22: 12). For the fourth time, Eliphaz stressed God's distance from man (cf. 4:17-19; 5:9; 15:14-16). In the face of such unfath-omable sovereignty, Job, according to Eliphaz, had the effrontery to say "What does God know? Can He judge through the thick darkness? Clouds are a hiding place for Him, so that He cannot

---

2. For example, Robert Gordis, *The Book of God and Man: A Study of Job,* p. 180.
3. Literally, "man of arm" and "lifted of face."

see; and He walks on the vault [dome][4] of heaven" (22:13-14).

Again Eliphaz trumped up a falsehood, for Job had never questioned God's omniscience (see 21:22). His justice, yes; but not His knowledge. In fact, God's awareness of all things—with apparent indifference—was what frustrated Job. Furthermore, Job had not questioned God's *ability* to judge; he challenged God's *failure* to judge. Also, Job had not said that God cannot see; he had said just the opposite (cf. 7:17-20).

Those misquotations were deliberately concocted to enable Eliphaz to have the upper hand in their dispute. Then Job's antagonist again assumed Job's sinful stance by asking if he intended to continue in his wrong direction: "Will you keep to the ancient path which wicked men have trod, who were snatched away before their time, whose foundations were washed away by a river?" (22:15-16). By this reference to the Flood, Eliphaz cruelly categorized Job with the wicked generation of Noah's day.

Then Eliphaz once more toyed with Job's words (21:14-16) and contorted them (22:17-18). Eliphaz sought to turn Job's very sentences around so that Job would seem to be a flagrant sinner ordering God to depart, even though God had made him prosper. Misquoting such irreverent expressions, however, caused Eliphaz to be repulsed, so he abruptly inserted the words, "the counsel of the wicked is far from me" (22:18b). These words had expressed Job's feelings (21:16) and here Eliphaz seemingly conveyed a double meaning, including a jest at Job's supposed dislike for the wicked and Eliphaz's own genuine disavowal of the advice of godless men.

Godly people see the judgment that comes to sinners "and are glad, and the innocent mock them," Eliphaz asserted (22:19). Sarcastically, Job had suggested they could mock on after he spoke (21:3), but Eliphaz took up the idea of mockery, affirming that the occasion for the mocking would be when the wicked, the adversaries of truth, were "cut off" and fire had burned up their wealth (22:20; cf. Bildad's reference to fire [15:34]).

d. *Eliphaz appealed to Job to repent* (22:21-30). Because Eliphaz's only explanation of Job's suffering was that he was

4. The word "dome" is literally "circle." The skies were considered the dome with which God covered the earth.

guilty of sin, the one solution was to repent. Even this appeal, though voiced in a kinder tone, assumed what Eliphaz could not prove—that Job was a sinner. The rigid theology of the three counselors had forced Eliphaz to a position of prevarication, a posture of groundless, homemade lies. For this reason his calm plea was not welcomed by the frantic, frustrated sufferer among the ashes.

Eliphaz's urgings included the following: (1) "yield" to God, which word in the Hebrew means "be intimately acquainted with" (which is precisely what Job wanted, so what good did Eliphaz's admonition do?); (2) "be at [make] peace with Him"; (3) "receive instruction from His mouth"; i.e., "be quiet and teachable while He instructs you";[5] (4) "establish His words in your heart"; i.e., assimilate God's commands in your life and obey them; (5) "return to the Almighty"; (6) "remove unrighteousness far from your tent"; i.e., abandon it rather than enjoy it (cf. Zophar's sentence about wickedness in Job's tent [11:14]); (7) "place your gold [literally, ore] in the dust, and the gold of Ophir[6] among the stones of the brooks," which clause probably means to renounce trust in material things.

If Job would meet those conditions, he would be assured of these results: (1) wealth ("good will come" [22:21], and "you will be restored" [22:23]); (2) spiritual fellowship ("the Almighty will be your gold and choice silver"; you "will delight" in Him; i.e., you will enjoy Him more than anything else; you will "lift up your face to God [boldly] . . . and He will hear you"; "you will [willingly] pay your vows"); (3) success (what you plan will be done and "light will shine on your ways"; i.e., you will have prosperity, success, and ease); (4) influence ("you will speak with confidence," and "God will save the humble and deliver the sinner because of your purity"[7]).

---

5. Eliphaz no doubt thought he was God's mouthpiece to whom Job should listen (see 4:12-21; 15:11).
6. On the southwestern coast of Arabia or in what is now Somaliland in Africa, but probably the former (cf. 28:16).
7. "Unconsciously he foretold what was to happen to him and his two friends (xlii. 8)," Victor E. Reichert, *Job,* p. 121.

2. *Job's third reply to Eliphaz* (chaps. 23—24)

Smarting under Eliphaz's nettling allegations, Job sensed a new level of desperation and frustration. And yet, rather than answer his plaintiff's accusations, Job turned to reflect in bitterness on two problems that continued to plague him: his own injustices and injustices in the world. His own injustices caused him to long for an opportunity to present his case to God (23:1-7), but God remained inaccessible in spite of Job's repeated claim of innocence (23:8-17). On the other hand, God, in response to the obvious wrongdoings of others, remained strangely inactive (24:1-25). Job's suffering, he felt, was undeserved, whereas others who did deserve punishment went scot-free; and both were clear cases of inequities met with divine silence.

a. *Job's longing* (23:1-7). Job knew that his complaint against God was a rebellious act and would be considered as such by Eliphaz and company, but he had unsuccessfully attempted to suppress his agony (23:2).[8] Eliphaz had urged the sufferer to "return to the Almighty" (22:23), but for Job that counsel was pointless. Job certainly wanted to turn to God, but there were two problems: he refused to confess sin of which he was not guilty, and he did not know where to find Him. God was apparently elusive, playing a cosmic game of hide and seek.[9] Yet Job desperately needed to find Him—for a personal appearance before God's judgment seat was apparently, Job felt, the only way he could acquire vindication from false charges and unfair treatment (23:3).

As his own defense attorney, Job said that he would present his case, arguing persuasively (23:4). Then he would listen to God's response (23:5), which would be far more accurate than the responses of the trio, for God, faced with the facts of Job's case, would have to admit to His injustice. "Would He contend with me?" asked Job. And answering his own question, he replied, "No, surely He would pay attention to me" (23:6). Previously Job had cited the uselessness of appearing before God

---

8. Instead of "His hand is heavy despite my groaning" (23:2) read "My hand is heavy upon my groaning."
9. L. D. Johnson, *Out of the Whirlwind: The Major Message of Job*, p. 47.

(9:14-16), but now he was convinced that God would not take advantage of His great power. There, at the divine tribunal, Job the upright would argue or reason with Him and he would finally and forever be delivered from injustice at the hands of his Judge (23:7).

b. *Job's innocence* (23:8-12). So certain was Job of the rightness of his position that he knew that God, who had been acting unfairly, would be forced to admit to justice and relieve Job. But there was one problem: his case could not be heard because the Judge would not appear in court!

Job then went on a massive God hunt to try to find the Judge. He moved in all directions—forward, backward, left, and right. These words suggested east, west, north, and south, for directions in the ancient Near East were determined from the perspective of a person facing east. No matter where Job investigated, God was not there or could not be seen (23:8-9). His search was in vain.

Verse 10a is usually taken to mean, "Though God eludes me, He does know about me." However, in the Hebrew the verse begins with "Because," so it should be understood as follows: "God is evading me *because* He knows my ways. He knows I am innocent and therefore is refusing to appear in court, for once He heard my case He would have to admit to injustice."

When God would appear in court and try Job's case, it would be evident, Job asserted, that he was gold and would shine[10] like it (23:10b).[11] No problem of low self-esteem here! No doubt the reference to gold was a retort to Eliphaz's earlier words about gold (22:25).

How could Job say that he would pass God's test and emerge as shining gold? Verses 11 and 12 affirm his faithful walk before God—again a refutation of the charges conjured by his garbage-heap grand jury!

Job was not following the ancient path of the wicked, as Eli-

10. "Shine" is a possible rendering instead of "come forth" in view of Ugaritic and Akkadian parallels (H. H. Rowley, *Job*, p. 172).
11. This meaning seems to be more accurate than the common view that Job was admitting to being tried for the purpose of coming forth from the testing more pure than before. Although trials may help to purify the believer's faith, like the burning of dross from gold (1 Pet 1:6-7), that does not seem to be what Job was saying here.

phaz has insinuated (22:15). Instead, his foot had followed in God's path of godliness; he had kept His way, and he had not deviated (23:11). Furthermore, Job need not start again to receive "instruction from His mouth," in accord with Eliphaz's advice (22:22), because Job had not departed from "the command of His lips." Instead, he had placed higher value on God's words than on daily food (23:12).

c. *Job's frustration* (23:13—24:17). Job complained that God terrified him (23:13-17); that God did not punish overt sinners (24:1-12); and that God did not punish covert sinners (24: 13-17). Job's desire for vindication in court and his inability to find God, linked with his awareness of a goldlike character, left two responses: exacerbation, and a realization of God's sovereignty. "He is unique," Job proclaimed (23:13).[12] Despite Job's bold demand for a court hearing, He had to admit that God could be restrained by no one, and that what God desires, He does. Job upstaged Eliphaz by pointing out that repentance would not make it possible for Job to have all his plans confirmed (22:28), because it was God who was carrying out in Job's life what *God* had decreed for him (23:14). This sense of God's mysterious uniqueness and irresistible ways led Job to a sense of dismay, terror, and faint-heartedness (23:15-16). Once again he recoiled from the notion of standing alone before God in self-defense. Even so, Job was not to be outdone by the darkness and deep gloom that were covering him (23:17; cf. 22:10-11).[13]

In chapter 24 Job was doing two things: lambasting God for being so apathetic toward injustice, and pointing Eliphaz to an even greater problem than the one Eliphaz had raised. That senior plaintiff had said that God was majestic and distant from man, but of greater concern to Job was God's apparent neglect to use that majesty to correct the world's wrongs. He wondered why God did not set aside specific times for judging so that those who trusted Him could see Him at work on those days (24:1).

12. Literally, "He is in one," meaning that He is in a class by Himself.
13. The Hebrew of this verse is difficult. It may mean that Job was dismayed because God had not cut him off (let him die) before his dark calamities came on him.

109

This is an understandable but strange inquiry in view of Job's previous statement that God is unique and does as He pleases.

In this section (24:2-12), Job mentioned three sins (24:2-4a); he described what happens to the victims of those crimes (24:4b-8); he referred again to the oppressors (24:9-10a); and he again discussed the victims (24:10b-12).

The three sins (24:2-4a) were removing landmarks, stealing, and mistreating the needy. Landmarks were boundary stones, marking off property lines. To move them was an attempt to enlarge one's property. Stealing flocks of sheep and then pasturing them as if they were one's own was theft, an obvious moral wrong. Mistreating the needy involved driving away donkeys that orphans were caring for (and because it would be impossible for children to chase and catch them, the loss would be irreparable), or taking a widow's ox as collateral on a loan, or pushing the needy off the road so that they could not even beg.

Pitiful results came to the victims of such thoughtless wrongdoings: They had to hide to escape more oppression, hunt for food in the desert like wild donkeys, gather fodder in the fields, work for the wicked by gleaning their vineyards, sleep with no protective clothing from the cold outdoors, suffer physically from being soaked by the heavy rains, and hug the rocks for shelter because of lack of houses (24:4b-8).

The ruthless people also stole fatherless babies from their mothers even while they were being fed, took pledges from the poor (thus further reducing the meager possessions of the poor), and stole clothing from the poor (24:9-10a). Job continued by saying that those helpless victims were forced to carry sheaves while going hungry, to produce oil by crushing olives within the walls (meaning, perhaps, between the rows of olive trees), and to tread grapes in the winepress while going thirsty (24:10b-11). Far from the city—out in the fields and in the deserts—the oppressed groan and cry for help, but "God does not pay attention to folly" (24:12). How God could be so oblivious to sins that He obviously sees committed in the open was difficult for Job to comprehend.

Then Job complained that God did not punish those who sin

secretly (24:13-17). Man may not see all that is done secretly in the dark by "those who rebel against the light" (24:13), but surely God does. Therefore, how can God withhold retribution? Murderers, adulterers, and housebreakers are not familiar with the light and do not "abide in its paths" because they do their sinister work at night. The murderer arises at night (24:14),[14] killing the poor and the needy, which is worse than the maligned treatment spoken of earlier (24:3-12), the adulterer waits until it is dark and also disguises himself (24:15); and the house thief does all his work at night (24:16-17).

d. *Job's confidence* (24:18-25). These verses seem to contradict what Job had said in the preceding verses. There he was upset because God did not do something to stop barbarous actions, but here he stated that God *does* punish the wicked. This problem has been handled in various ways. Some writers suggest that these are Zophar's words (he did not speak a third time, so this would give him a third speech, though out of order before Bildad's third speech). Other writers put the words in the mouth of Bildad. Still other writers, following the principle of quotations, introduce the passage with the words "You say," and put 24:18-20 in quotation marks. That way Job was quoting one of the three counselors in order to rebut them (24:21-25). (Or, Job quoted one of the three friends in 24:18-24 and gave his response in 24:25). Still another view is that Job spoke the words, recognizing that the wicked do eventually come to death and are forgotten. Andersen, in suggesting this view, writes that Job never said that the wicked do *not* suffer. Instead, Job said that *both* the righteous and the wicked suffer, and *both* prosper.[15] This idea is far different from the limited, truncated theology of the three friends, who adamantly insisted that only the wicked suffer and only the righteous prosper. Yet this view was part of Job's bafflement with the world's injustice.

The view that verses 18-25 are Job's words deserves consideration. Viewed in that way, Job affirmed that the oppressors became as insignificant as foam or something lightweight on the sur-

14. The Hebrew of "at dawn" can mean "at the close of the light," i.e., at night.
15. Francis I. Andersen, *Job: An Introduction and Commentary*, pp. 213-14.

face of the water and that their land was cursed and therefore nonproductive (24:18). Consequently they would perish in Sheol much like the snow that is melted by the drought and heat and then evaporates (24:19). The womb that bore the wicked person would forget him, and only the worm feeding on his decaying body would remember him. His wickedness would be cut off abruptly, like a tree that is felled (24:20).

The wicked person who wronged the barren women or the widow would be dragged off by God, who when He judges causes people to have no confidence that they will live (24:21-22). Although it may appear that God is giving the wicked security, Job said, His eyes are on them (24:23). They may be in high positions of wealth and power, but then they are gone, debased, and gathered up like heads of grain and cut off (24:24).

Seeing these verses as Job's words is consistent with his earlier perturbation (24:1-17) over God's seeming permission of injustices. Here his concern was that the wicked were provided "with security" and were "exalted a little while." The friends had affirmed that the wicked were cut off immediately, but Job's view of reality did not confirm their doctrine. To him, the wicked were secure and exalted (though eventually they died), and that was seeming injustice.

The final verse in this oration (24:25), was Job's challenge to the three friends to prove him wrong and an underscoring of the certainty of his view.

10

Not Guilty!

3. *Bildad's third speech* (chap. 25)

Bildad's unusually brief lecture may well indicate that the three counselors were running out of arguments with which to respond to Job. No wonder, for their theology was rather one-tracked.

Because of the brevity of Bildad's speech and the absence of a third speech by Zophar, many attempts have been made to add to Bildad's speech by taking from Job's words in chapter 26 and/or 27. Those efforts will be discussed later in connection with chapters 26—31. There seems to be no adequate reason to add to Bildad's speech, which is self-contained, which dramatizes his lack of arguments, and which provides a striking literary contrast to Job's lengthy speech in chapters 26—31.

Compared with his other two spiels (chaps. 8, 18), this one began without reproving Job for his useless words. Also his subject this time was different; rather than harping on the downfall of the wicked, he accentuated the insignificance and iniquity of all men. Was he silenced on the theme of God's judgment on the ungodly by Job's realistic picture of the delay of such punishment (chap. 24)? If so, his response is a last-ditch effort to say something, to avoid admitting defeat—and yet an endeavor to use Job's own words about man (25:4; cf. 9:2b) to bring him to see his sin, and an endeavor to use Job's own concept about God's sovereignty to demonstrate how useless it is for a person to attempt a hearing in court with God.

Ignoring Job's concern for God's indifference to injustice, Bildad sought to go a step higher on the ladder of debate by extolling God's greatness. He said that God rules and that His sovereign rule results in respect ("dominion and awe belong to Him"). Furthermore, God establishes order (or harmony) in the heavens (25:2). So great is He that His troops (referring to angels, or possibly stars, although the stars are referred to separately [25:5]) are numberless, and His light penetrates to all persons and places (25:3).

Bildad's first rhetorical question, "How then can a man be just with God?" (25:4a) repeated Eliphaz's earlier words (4: 17a). Bildad also quoted Job, who had asked that same question (9:2b). The second rhetorical question, "How can he be clean who is born of a woman?" (25:4b) was similar to Eliphaz's earlier words (4:17b; 15:14). Perhaps by going back to an original theme, he hoped to be able to cinch the matter with Job. The entire human race is unclean spiritually, so surely Job would get the subtle suggestion that he was included! Bildad excluded any reference to man's becoming right with God or pure.

The argument Bildad used next (25:5-6) was also aimed at belittling Job. Because the moon and stars, which in all their great distance, brilliance, and awesomeness, are only insignificant luminaries, surely man ("man" here is the word for weak man; the "son of man" suggests man's creation out of dust) is puny physically and putrid as worms spiritually. The moon only reflects light, and the stars "are not pure in His sight," meaning that they are not bright in comparison with God. Eliphaz had contrasted man with the angels (4:18-19; 15:15-16), and Bildad now contrasted man with the moon and stars. Referring to man as a maggot, the word for putrefying worms, would have had an unusual wallop against Job, because as he had said, "My flesh is clothed with worms" (7:5). The second Hebrew word for worm in 25:6 suggests the weakness of the worm.

By calling attention to God's majesty, and to the moon, man, and maggots, Bildad sought to get Job to face up to the reality of his own worthlessness. Job of course had no quarrel with the majesty of God, but the rest of Bildad's speech was pointless, because it gave no hope for vindication, which Job craved, and no hope for purification, which Job had already said he did not need. "On this disgusting and hopeless note the words of Job's friends end."[1]

1. Francis I. Andersen, *Job: An Introduction and Commentary*, p. 215.

4. *Job's third reply to Bildad* (chaps. 26—31)

These chapters constitute Job's longest speech, although some scholars reduce its length by assigning 26:5-14 to Bildad or 27: 7-23 or 27:13-23 to Zophar or Bildad.[2] If chapters 26—31 were all spoken by Job, they constitute a fitting contrast to the brevity of Bildad's third speech (chap. 25). Chapter 26 is a reply to Bildad ("you" in 26:2-4 is singular), but it is clear that in chapters 27—31 Job replies in a grand finale to all three contestants ("you" in 27:5, for example, is plural). In this concluding response, Job includes a disclaimer of Bildad's wisdom (chaps. 26—27) and a discourse on God's wisdom (chap. 28), and he then climaxes his speech with a desire for his past glory (chap. 29), a dirge regarding his present misery (chap. 30), and a declaration of his innocence (chap. 31).

a. *Job's disclaimer of Bildad's wisdom* (chaps. 26—27). Chapter 26 is in two parts: Job's rebuke of Bildad's attitude (26: 1-4) and Job's statement of God's greatness (26:5-14). In stunning fashion, Job turned both aspects of Bildad's argument against him. Bildad had affirmed that man, including Job, was puny and corrupt; Job retorted that Bildad was the puny one (26: 2-4). Also Bildad had stated that God was majestic; Job responded with statements about God's majesty that were far more majestic than Bildad's (26:5-14). Then in the next chapter Job touched again on two related themes: He repudiated Bildad's "worm analysis" of man by reaffirming his own innocence (27: 1-6), and he enlarged on Bildad's view of God by declaring that God would, in time, destroy the wicked (27:7-23).

Job's rejoinder to Bildad (26:1-4) is "dripping with irony."[3] In sarcastic indignation, Job fired back at Bildad. Bildad had viewed Job as one with no power ("weak"), no strength, and no wisdom. Why then had he not helped him, supported him, and counseled him? (This may also be a subtle slam at Eliphaz's earlier words [4:3-4]). Speaking of the "helpful insight" Bildad had "abundantly provided" (26:3b), Job was no doubt sarcas-

---

2. These suggestions are discussed later in connection with the commentary on 26:5 and 27:13.
3. L. D. Johnson, *Out of the Whirlwind: The Major Message of Job*, p. 49.

tically blasting Bildad's short speech, which was given without help, without insight, and without kindness.

"To whom" (26:4) may be understood as "From whom," the thought being "Who helped you utter these words?" The clear implication is, "No one would help you say such things. You can't help others, and no one helps you. These are obviously your own inventions, and are thus worthless."

Job added, furthermore, that Bildad could lay no claim to having spoken words inspired by some other source such as God or wise men (26:4b). In present-day vernacular, he was speaking off the top of his head.

Verses 5-14 of chapter 26 are ascribed by some commentators to Bildad and by others to Zophar. However, the stabbing effect of Bildad's closing words (25:6) is lost if 26:5-14 is added to them. Also, "26:2-4 makes sense as Job's retaliation to this insult, but it is inconceivable that Job would heap scorn on such a superb exposition of God's splendour as 26:5-14, if this is Bildad's final word."[4] Bildad's and Zophar's emphases (chaps. 8; 11; 18; 20; 25) had been on the sinner's fate, with comparatively little emphasis on God's majesty, whereas Job had spoken repeatedly of the greatness of God (e.g., 9:4-10; 12:13-25). The words here (26:5-14) are more fitting for Job than for either Bildad or Zophar. It is typical of Job to outdo his friends-turned-rivals in his understanding of God's transcendence.

Bildad had spoken of angels (25:3), and had said that the heavens were impure (25:5) and man was a worm (25:6).[5] Job, in contrast enunciated God's grandeur over various parts of the universe. This passage is a resplendent mosaic of God's superiority over cosmology. Job referred to death, outer space, the earth, clouds, the moon, the waters, light, darkness, mountains, the sea, and the heavens. God's relationship to all these elements—from Sheol beneath to outer space above—includes His knowledge, creative design and power, providential control, and omnipotent supremacy.

---

4. Andersen, p. 216.
5. Interestingly, Eliphaz had spoken along similar lines: the angels are inadequate (5:1; 15:15a), the heavens are impure (15:15b), and man is impure (4:17; 15:14).

The term "departed spirits" (26:5) translates a Hebrew word that means "giants" and is elsewhere translated "Rephaim" (Gen 14:5; 15:20; Deut 2:11, 20; 3:11, 13; Josh 12:4; 13:12; 17:15). In Ugaritic the term meant the chief gods or aristocratic warriors, both of which groups may have seemed giantlike in their power. When it referred to the dead, the word seemed to take on the meaning of "the elite among the dead" (cf. Psalm 88:10; Prov 2:18; 9:18; 21:16; Isa 14:9; 26:14, 19).[6] Job's point here (26:5) is that even the elite who are dead tremble under God's authority. Those people who are in Sheol and Abaddon, a poetic synonym of Sheol,[7] are known to God even though, as conceived in ancient times, the place of the dead was understood to be "under the waters."

God's creation of the skies was likened by Job to His stretching out a tent on a pole. The "north" is the celestial pole around which the universe appears to revolve.[8] The earth was viewed by Job as being supported by nothing material and therefore as being sustained only by God.

Although the water in the sky is collected in clouds, as in bottles or waterskins, yet the clouds, suspended in air, do not burst with the weight of the water (26:8; cf. 38:37). This is a remarkable feat, unachievable by man. God can even use the clouds to obscure the full moon (26:9).

Then comes the third reference to "waters" in this short passage (26:10; the other references are 26:5, 8). God has drawn "a circle on the surface of the waters [unto] the boundary [confines] of light and darkness." The "circle" may refer to the horizon, which appears to be circular, where light and darkness begin

---

6. Conrad L'Heureux, "The Ugaritic and Biblical Rephaim," *Harvard Theological Review* 67 (1974):265-74.
7. Abaddon, meaning a place of or the condition of destruction, is used only six times in the Old Testament: 26:6; 28:22; 31:12; Psalm 88:11, marg.; Prov 15:11; 27:20.
8. Some writers see in the word for "north" (*Zaphon*) a reference to the cosmic mountain, Mount Zaphon, where the gods of Canaanite mythology assembled (cf. Isa 14:13), or a mountain in Canaanite Syria. Isaiah 14:13 uses the word *Zaphon* to refer to God's abode, thus indicating that what was a mere mountain in pagan mythology was the majestic heavens in divine cosmology. Verse 7 thus becomes a polemic against the Canaanite myth.

and end, as the sun rises in the east and sets in the west. Or the "circle" may refer to the dome-shaped outline of the sky, which includes the luminaries (sun, moon, and stars), and beyond which all is darkness; thus the circle was the boundary line where light terminated in darkness. The earth was thought to be surrounded by waters; the domed sky was above, and beyond the dome was God's dwelling (22:14; Isa 40:22).

"The pillars of heaven" (26:11) refers to the mountains that support the sky (cf. 9:6). Though strong they "tremble" and "are amazed" (are astounded) when God's voice rebukes them, that is, when He brings thunder, storms, wind, and/or earthquakes (cf. Psalms 18:7; 104:32; Nah 1:5).

Job then speaks of God's control over the raging sea (26:12-13). As seen earlier in the book (7:12; 9:13), the Hebrew word for "sea" (*yam*) may allude to the Ugaritic sea god Yam defeated by Baal or to the Mesopotamian sea monster Tiamat defeated by Marduk. Rahab (26:12*b*) is another name for that sea god, and the "fleeing serpent" (26:13) may possibly refer to the same monster (which is identified with Leviathan [Isa 27:1]). Job's use of these mythological terms in no way suggests that he believed in the existence of those gods. Instead, the terms point polemically to God's supremacy as the *only* God—the all-powerful One, who can conquer all alleged pagan deities. "It is true that . . . to quell the sea is a natural figure, but it is perhaps more likely . . . that Job celebrates the power of God in conquering the evil and proud mythological deities of the heathen."[9]

The word "quieted" (26:12) is rendered by some versions as "stirred up." However, "quieted" means "to make afraid" and thus "to restrain," which fits the context (26:12-13). "By His breath the heavens are cleared" (26:13*a*), refers to the wind by which God clears the sky of clouds after a storm.[10] "His hand has pierced the fleeing serpent" (26:13*b*), parallels "And by His

---

9. R. Laird Harris, "The Book of Job and Its Doctrine of God," *Grace Journal* 13 (Fall 1976): 20.

10. N. H. Tur-Sinai (*The Book of Job: A New Commentary* [Jerusalem: Kiryath-Sepher (1957], p. 384) renders 26:13*a* "By His wind He put the sea in a bag." He does this by dividing the words for "heavens" into two words ("put" and "sea") and by taking the word for "are cleared" as "a bag." Although there may be some support for this, it seems tenuous.

understanding He shattered [literally smote, or wounded] Rahab" (26:12*b*).

Job concluded his grand exposition of God's evidences of His power over nature (below, above, and on the earth) by stating that these examples are only "the fringes of His ways"; that is, they are only the outer extremities or outlines of God's actions. God's power over and knowledge of Sheol, His creation of outer space and the earth, His control of the clouds, His demarcating of the realms of light and darkness, His shaking of the mountains, His quelling of the sea, His destruction of alleged opposing deities—to call these accomplishments the bare outlines or fragmentary sketches of God's activities gives an awareness of the vast immensity and incomprehensible infinity of God! In fact, Job added, man is so remote from God that he hears only a faint whisper of what God says. Even if God were to speak from the thunder of His power (rather than in a whisper) man still could not understand. No man can fully comprehend God's activities or His power. Surely Job's awareness of God's awesome nature exceeded Bildad's sense of God's power. In the next section (27:1-6), Job again affirmed his innocence. "Then Job continued his discourse and said" (27:1), may suggest that Job paused, waiting for Zophar to answer. Then when Zophar remained silent, Job continued. And here he addressed all three companions ("you" [27:5, 11, 12] is plural).

Job introduced his statement of innocence with an oath, "As God lives," thus asserting that what he was about to affirm was as certain as God's existence. Job realized the paradox of such a strong adjuration, because that very living God had "taken away [his] right" (i.e., his cause) by refusing to hear his case, and had "embittered [his] soul" (cf. 7:11; 9:18; 10:1). Although Job said that God was unjust to him (6:4; 7:20; 10:2-3; 13:24; 16:12-13; etc.), he could appeal to no higher tribunal. "Once more, the two conceptions of God, against whom and to whom he appeals, lie side by side in Job's thought."[11] Job and his pugilists were locked in an irresolvable conflict, but the debate regarding Job's rightness or wrongness could be settled only by God.

11. H. H. Rowley, *Job*, p. 220.

Job's statement of innocence (27:3-6) includes several negatives and one positive. Job said that for as long as he lived,[12] he would not be untruthful and deceiving in what he said ("speak unjustly" is literally "speak falsehood") (27:3-4). Therefore, to declare the three comforters to be right in their accusations would be impossible (27:5a). His wife had urged him to put away his integrity and die (2:9), but Job affirmed that until his death he would not do such a thing. Instead, he would hold fast his righteousness (this word is related to the word "right" [27:5]), and his heart, probably meaning his conscience, would not reproach (speak sharp, accusing things to) him as long as he lived (27:6). This strongly worded oath of innocence is consistent with Job's former assertions of not-guilty in response to Eliphaz (6:10, 29-30; 16:17; 23:10-12), Bildad (9:35; 10:7), and Zophar (12:4; 13:18-19).

Job began recounting the fate of the wicked man (27:7-23) by desiring that his enemies be like the wicked and the unjust, not in character, but in their fate (27:7). Thus it is evident that Job did not consider himself among the wicked or the guilty. If a plaintiff made an accusation that turned out to be false, he himself was subject to the penalty of the crime wrongly charged. In a series of three questions (27:8-10) Job pointed out that the godless (irreligious) man has no hope when God cuts him off and takes his soul, the godless man has no answer to his cries for help in time of distress (the word "distress" refers to a narrow place and thus a difficult situation), and the godless man will not delight in God the Almighty nor continually call on God, thus showing that he is not truly a godly person.

In 27:10 Job turned the suggestion of Eliphaz (22:20-27) back on him, and in 27:11 Job reversed Eliphaz's suggestion. The latter had urged Job to receive instruction from God, but Job said he would instruct Eliphaz and his friends regarding God's power and would teach them things about the Almighty.[13] Even so, his

---

12. 'Life' (27:3a) is literally "breath"; and "breath of God" (27:3b), while literally "spirit of God," is probably to be understood as another synonym for "breath" because of the reference to the nostrils.
13. Job employed several words for God in interesting fashion: El ("God"), Shaddai ("Almighty"), and Eloah ("God") (27:2-3); Eloah and El (27:8-9); Shaddai, Eloah, El, and Shaddai, in that order (27:10-11), and El and Shaddai (27:13).

teaching would be only reminders of what they already knew about God. Therefore, it was the height of foolishness for them to accuse him of sin, thus risking the fate of the wicked on themselves.

Many writers view the next section (27:13-23) as the words of Zophar because (1) Job, in speaking here of the fate of the wicked, would seem to be contradicting his earlier words (9:22-24; 21:7-34; 24:18-24), (2) giving Zophar a third speech would complete the balanced structure of the cycle of speeches, (3) several statements in this passage are similar to Zophar's previous words (cf. 27:13 with 20:29; 27:14 with 20:10, 21, 26, 28; 27:16-17 with 20:15, 18, 21, 28; 27:18 with 20:28; 27:20 with 20:8, 25c, 28b; and 27:23 with 20:8).

However, seeing the section as Job's is to be preferred for these reasons: (1) the section is consistent with Job's imprecatory desire that his enemy (the three friends considered collectively) become "as the wicked" (27:7-10). (2) Job had never denied that the wicked will *eventually* be punished; he only questioned why they continue to prosper. This idea is similar to Jobs' previous words (24:18-25). The *ultimate* judgment of the wicked contrasts with the *immediate* and sudden destruction of the wicked, which Zophar had expounded (chap. 20). (3) The fact that several statements in 27:13-23 are similar to Zophar's words in chapter 20 could just as easily argue for their being Job's words. Frequently, Job threw the friends' arguments back on them by using their own words. What more effective way to accuse them of being wicked than to employ against them their own words about the fate of the wicked? (4) The absence of a speech by Zophar is consistent with the fact that the speeches of the three friends become progressively shorter, and it suggests Job's verbal victory over Zophar. (5) Chapter 28 appears to be a continuation of 27:13-23, thus suggesting the same speaker. But chapter 28 is inappropriate for Zophar.

The passage is introduced (27:13) in words very similar to Zophar's earlier words (20:29). Job then spoke of the wicked person's loss of his children (27:14-15) and wealth (27:16-23). He said that the wicked tyrant's children may be numerous, but

121

they would be killed in war and his descendants would suffer famine (27:14). If any survived war or famine, he would die of the plague; and the widows would not mourn for their dead husbands (either because they would not be permitted to mourn in times of disaster or because the wicked dead would be undeserving of mourning).

The wealth of the wicked would be lost, Job asserted (27:16-23). Although they pile up silver like dust and prepare (literally, stack up) garments like clay (both are figures of plenitude, for dust and clay were common!), the wicked would be unable to enjoy them, for their silver and garments would pass into the hands of the righteous and the innocent (who are often equated with the poor) (27:16-17).

His house, supposedly strong and secure, would be as unstable as a moth's cocoon or a watchman's hut (27:18). The latter was a temporary shelter made at harvest time by a farmer so that he could take shelter in it or guard the orchard or vineyard. Job continued by saying that one day the wicked man is rich, but the next day, when he wakes up, all his wealth is gone (27:19). Not only would his possessions be taken, but also he himself would be gone. He would suddenly be overtaken by a terrifying flood, a tempest (windstorm) would snatch him away in the night, and the east wind (the strong, dry wind—known as the sirocco— from the east desert) would carry him and whirl him away. Any attempt to escape would be in vain. The wind is personified as clapping its hands and hissing from its place in derisive mockery at the wicked man, who thought that his wealth gave him security (27:23). The clapping and hissing, in addition to referring figuratively to the contemptuous treatment given the wicked, may also include a subtle reference to the noise of the wind.

b. *Job's discourse on God's wisdom* (chap. 28). Many scholars assign this chapter to Zophar, Bildad, or even God, or treat it as a poem that was not part of the book of Job originally. It does seem to be unrelated to what precedes and follows it, and it is in a different mood, but the subject matter—man's inability to discover God's wisdom—is in keeping with Job's words (26:14, as well as 9:10-12; 12:13; 17:10; 23:8-10).[14] This chapter is fittingly Job's, for he had been refuting the three counselors, who had maintained that they knew God's ways. Job now affirmed that it is not possible for man to presume that he can discern the inscrutable mysteries of the majestic God. As Michaelis states so clearly:

> But to man this wisdom [by which God made and governs all things] must remain inscrutable. To him God said: Trouble not thyself with inquiring how I govern the world; why I permit the tyrant to be victorious, or innocence and truth to be oppressed: decide not what evil I can or cannot suffer to exist in the world. This is too high for thee: let thy wisdom consist in fearing me, upon whose will all things depend. . . .[15]

Man, in spite of his engineering skills (28:1-11), cannot discover or purchase wisdom (28:12-22); only God knows where true wisdom is to be found (28:23-28). Job spoke of the metals (silver, gold, iron, copper, and precious stones) that are mined by man (28:1-2, 6), and he spoke of the ingenious ways by which the metals and stones are discovered beneath the surface of the earth (28:3-5, 7-11). Silver was mined in Arabia (2 Chron 9:14) and Tarshish (Jer 10:9), gold was imported from Arabia (2 Chron 9:14) including Ophir (1 Kings 10:11) and Sheba (1 Kings 10:2).

The mining shafts bring light to the dark recesses of mines (28:3), where people have never lived (28:4). Miners, forgotten by people walking above the mine, hang and dangle, apparently while being lowered by ropes into mining holes far below the sight of men on the surface (28:4).[16] From the surface

14. Andersen's view that chapter 28 is an interlude written by the author of the book (thus serving as a transition from the three rounds of dialogues to the three rounds of monologues by Job, Elihu, and Jehovah) is intriguing, but it (1) does not explain why 29:1 states that "Job again took up his discourse," (2) overlooks similarities between chapter 28 and Job's words elsewhere (e.g., 28:24-27 and 26:5-13), (3) does not account for the possibility that Job may have changed from speaking about the wealth of the wicked (chap. 27) to man's ability to unearth much of that wealth (chap. 28), (4) disregards Job's continued frustration with and recognition of his inability to discover God's ways, and (5) assumes an author outside the circle of the five major conversants in the book.

15. J. D. Michaelis, quoted by E. P. Barrows, "Interpretation of the Twenty-Eighth Chapter of Job," *Bibliotheca Sacra* 10 (1853):271.

16. This is one way of understanding this verse. Numerous other renderings of the obscure Hebrew are revealed by a glance at various versions.

of the earth comes food (from vegetative growth), but from beneath the surface "it is turned up as fire" (28:5). This latter clause may mean that "the overturning that goes on underground produces confused rubble like that caused by fire,"[17] or that the precious stones that are disclosed by the overturning of the earth seem to glow like fire,[18] or that the ore-containing rocks had been produced by volcanic fire[19] or mine blasting. The first of these views seems preferable. The sapphires mentioned next (28:6) are lapis lazuli, the ore of which contains particles that look like gold. The inaccessibility of the mines to animals is then specified: birds of prey with keen insight like the falcon, lions ("proud beasts" probably means lions) with their courage, and serpents[20] with their sly movements are unable to see or touch what man does in mining (28:7-8). The falcon is above the earth, the lion on the earth, and the serpent in it.

Verses 9-11, like verses 3-4, speak of man's mining operations. He breaks through solid rock, overturns mountains at their base (literally, by the roots), cuts channels (tunnels) in the rocks, and is thus enabled to see valuable metals. In addition, he dams up underground streams so that they do not trickle or seep into the mine and thus hamper his mining operations.

All this activity results in his bringing to light the metals and stones that were hidden in the darkness.

In spite of man's technological abilities to mine precious stones and ores that lie beyond the sight of man, bird, and beast, he cannot find wisdom (28:12). Its value is unknown, its location has not been found in all "the land of the living" (the inhabited earth), in the deep waters beneath the earth, or in the sea. Not only can man not find wisdom, he cannot even purchase it with the precious metals he has found (28:15-19). Job used almost a dozen different words for various metals, including three words that are found only here in the Old Testament ("pure gold,"

17. Rowley, p. 228.
18. Albert Barnes, *Notes, Critical, Illustrative, and Practical, on the Book of Job*, 2:64.
19. Marvin H. Pope, *Job*, p. 201.
20. Sigmund Mowinckel suggests that the mythological griffin (lion-dragon) is suggested here (*Hebrew and Semitic Studies*, ed. D. Winton Thomas and W. D. McHardy [Oxford: Clarendon, 1963], pp. 95-103).

"glass," and "crystal"); the meanings of those three words are therefore difficult to know with precision. Verse 20 is almost identical with verse 12, and verses 21 and 22 are close in thought to verses 13 and 14. As the deep and the sea (28:14) were personified, saying that wisdom is not in them, so Abaddon (a synonym for Sheol; it is used three times by Job in his closing oration; cf. 26:6; 31:12) and Death stated that they have heard rumors about wisdom, the implication being that they do not possess it and know little about it (28:22).

Job concludes the chapter (28:23-28) by answering the questions "Where can wisdom be found?" (28:12) and "Where then does wisdom come from?" (28:20). By being first in the sentence in Hebrew, the word "God" (Elohim) is emphasized (28:23). Only God knows where wisdom is to be found (28:23), for He alone is omniscient (28:24). His looking "to the ends of the earth" and His seeing "everything under the heavens," all in one immediate glance, contrast sharply with man's laborious searching and probing for wisdom without finding it and with the inability of even "birds of the sky," with their vast sweep of vision, to see it (28:7, 21).

Job's appreciation of God's sovereignty over and providential care for His creation is again seen in His establishment of regulations that govern four aspects of nature (28:25-26). Although storms appear to be without order, their elements were determined by His wise, creative genius. The weight (i.e., force) of the wind, the measure (i.e., amount) of water, a limit (literally, decree, law, rule, regulation) for the rain (thus indicating that rain is not haphazard or by chance), and the path followed by the thunderbolt—all were determined by God.

When God, in His creative work, prescribed laws for the wind, waters, rain, and lightning, He explored wisdom, which is treated as a tangible object or idea (28:27). (Cf. Prov 8:27-30, which is strikingly similar.) He saw it, probed it (a possible rendering for the word "declared"), established it, and investigated it. Together these verbs suggest that He perfectly fathomed the nature of wisdom—in stark contrast to man's inability even to *find* it. The verb "established" may point to His setting forth laws regarding the relationship of wisdom to man. The necessity of

125

divine, propositional revelation is indicated next: "to man He said" (28:28). Although man is impotent to discover or purchase wisdom, he can know its very essence, for God has unveiled what otherwise would remain "hidden from the eyes of all living" (28:21). That essence of wisdom is twofold, "the fear of the Lord [Adonai]" and "to depart from evil."

All man's scientific investigations, technological advances, and intellectual achievements—remarkable as they are, whether in Job's day or the present—fail miserably to provide "a full explanation of [God's] government [or to] disclose all that we would wish to know about God."[21] Instead, real wisdom consists in establishing one's life in submissive veneration before God, in revering God in an attitude of confidence that He does all things right (although that rightness may not always be apparent to man). True wisdom also consists in a rejection of evil, in a regulating of one's conduct in paths of piety, and in actions and attitudes that accord with God's standards of holiness and godliness. Fearing God and turning from evil may be summarized as adoration of God and obedience to God. Thus the truly wise man is the one whose life is centered on God, not self, and is regulated by God. Man in right relationship to God, worshiping Him, serving Him, obeying Him—*that* is wisdom and understanding!

This chapter may be seen as Job's rebuke to the shortsighted wisdom of his antagonists,[22] an effort to demonstrate that their limited theological outlook was false. Seen as a disclaimer to their accusations that he was not fearing God and needed to turn from evil, the chapter is unquestionably fitting as the words of Job. Also, it is consistent with God's earlier assessment of Job (1:1, 8; 2:3), thus demonstrating to the reader that the three friends were mistaken in their demand that Job must begin to revere God and repent of sin. Chapter 28 argues that he had been fearing God and hating evil, but that they had not! Seen in this way, the final verse of the chapter becomes "one of the great, climactic moments in the Book."[23]

21. Barnes, 2:73.
22. Gleason L. Archer, Jr., *A Survey of Old Testament Introduction* (Chicago: Moody, 1964), p. 447.
23. Victor E. Reichert, *Job,* p. 145.

126

The closing verse of chapter 28 also serves as an apposite link to chapters 29—31. In chapter 29 Job rehearsed his past virtues—evidences that he feared God; and in chapter 31 he recounted his innocence with regard to numerous sins—evidences that he turned from evil.

c. *Job's desire for his past glory* (chap. 29). In the three final chapters of Job's last speech, he gave a concluding summary of his case, as if he were in court. He reviewed the past blessings he enjoyed and the reasons for them (chap. 29), he bemoaned his present miseries (chap. 30), and he pronounced an oath of innocence (chap. 31). This concluding soliloquy makes no mention of the three friends, which is also true of Job's opening soliloquy (chap. 3). In his first outcry, Job had said that he longed to die, but in the last one he said that he would die under God's cruelty (30:21-23). Nevertheless, in a bold dash of confidence he made one last plea for God to hear him in court (31:35-37).

In chapter 29 Job expressed his longing for his former days of prosperity and happiness (29:1-11) and then spelled out his reasons for having enjoyed those blessings (29:12-25). Those were his autumn days (29:4, marg.), when he was in mature adulthood. The opening verse is identical to 27:1, again suggesting a continuation after a pause for a reply. Remarkably, his former enjoyment of fellowship with God is the first thing he mentioned. The sense that God had now left him was more painful than his other miseries, especially in view of his former fellowship. "Months gone by" (29:2) suggests that several months have passed since disaster had struck. It may have taken a few weeks for Job's comforters to arrange to meet him. His former fellowship with God included God's guarding care (29:2b), His blessings ("His lamp shone over my head" [29:3a]), His guidance through difficulties (29:3b), His friendship (the word suggests intimate companionship [29:4]), and His presence (29:5a). In his predisaster days, Job had also had his children with him (29:5b), and he was unusually prosperous (butter and oil were symbols of plenty)[24] (29:6). In addition, he enjoyed social prestige (29:7-11). He was a local judge (city

24. The rock pouring out streams of oil may refer to the olive press or to the rocky soil in which olive trees grow.

elders would hold court sessions and conduct other public business at the city gate—does this account for Job's frequent use of legal terms?), respected not only by young men but even by men older than himself, an unusual phenomenon (29:7-8). Out of respect and a desire to hear him speak, princes and nobles (city officials of varying ranks) became quiet in his presence (29:9-10). On hearing Job's opinion, the officials commended him, and their fixed attention on him reflected their respect and admiration for him (29:11).

The blessing of God and the respect of the community leaders were his for several reasons (introduced by "because" [29:12]): he helped others (29:12-13), he exercised justice (29:14-20), he gave wise counsel (29:21-25). As a champion of the underdog, he gave help, which included financial assistance and/or release from unfair oppression, to the poor and to orphans. He helped those who were on the brink of despair, and their relief caused them to bless him (29:13a); and he encouraged despondent, grieving widows to the extent that they sang for joy (29:13b).

His exercise of justice was so consistent and so evident that they were like a robe and a turban (29:14). He assisted people who were handicapped by blindness or lameness, he provided for the needy as if he were their father, and he was concerned that justice be given even to those who were complete strangers to him (29:15-16). There may be irony here in that whereas he did those things for the needy, neither his three assailants nor God were returning that kind of justice to him. His justice was twofold: fairness and assistance to the injured, and punishment to the oppressor (29:17). Breaking "the jaws of the wicked" and snatching "the prey from his teeth" suggest a man's defeat of an animal that was ready to devour the victim it had in its mouth.

Having such selfless benevolence and equitable justice, Job said that he expected to continue with God's blessings on him right up to his death: he would have his nest (i.e., his children) around him and he would have longevity. He enjoyed refreshing stability (his root below ground spread out to the waters), prosperity (dew was on his branches above), glory (perhaps that word means "an enviable reputation"), and strength (the bow was a symbol of strength, and its being renewed in the hand suggested perennial strength (29:18-20).

The respect shown to Job by those whom he counseled was of the highest order, and contrasted keenly with the disrespect of the three disputants who had come to console. In former days, Job's counselees listened (29:21); they had nothing more to say, apparently because they were helped by his advice and respected the wisdom of it (29:22); and they eagerly anticipated his counsel, as if they were crops waiting for the necessary spring rain (29:23). He encouraged them by his smile and was not in turn made despondent by their despondency (29:24). He told his counselees the course of action to take, which they presumably followed implicitly and respectfully, for he was like a chief and a king giving directions. His counseling services also included giving comfort for those who grieved (29:25)—something in which his three companions were disappointingly remiss.

d. *Job's dirge on his present misery* (chap. 30). In chapter 30 Job turned to his present state ("now" introduces three of the four paragraphs in the chapter [30:1, 9, 16]) to describe an almost incredible reversal of attitude and experience. Chapter 29 speaks of what the Lord gave to Job and chapter 30 speaks of what the Lord took away (cf. 1:21). He was disrespected by low-class youth rather than honored by nobility (30:1-15), he was disregarded by God rather than blessed by Him (30:16-23), and he was despondent in his intense physical and emotional pain (30:24-31). This chapter is a poignant cry of one who was acutely miserable socially, spiritually, emotionally, and physically.

The indignities Job said he received from low-class, starving urchins (30:1-15) contrasted strikingly with the respect shown to him and his counsel by others, including even older men (29: 8, 21-25). Having had "the respect of the most respectable," he now had "the contempt of the most contemptible"[25] (cf. 19: 18). Job described who they were (scum [30:1-8]), and what

25. Andersen, p. 235.

129

they did (scorn, [30:9-15]). Because elders were to be highly respected in the ancient Near East, and particularly a man of social, economic, and spiritual stature like Job, the scorn he received from those younger than him was especially painful. To be disgraced by peers or superiors would be distressing enough, but he was derided by those who were so low that he would not even put their fathers with the dogs of his flock (30:1)! This is especially sarcastic in view of the fact that dogs were considered to be the lowest of animals because of their scavengerlike, wild behavior. Job described the ragamuffins as (1) useless and weak (30:2), (2) thin from famine and thus acting like animals gnawing the ground in an effort to get food (30:3), (3) forced to eat mallow (a plant with sour-tasting leaves, growing in salty marshes) and broom-shrub roots (also very bitter in taste)—plants that only the most abject poor would resort to for food (30:4), (4) expelled from normal society as if they were thieves (30:5), (5) dwelling in the desert in dry wadis, holes, and caves (30:6), (6) sounding like wild donkeys ("cry out" is the word "bray") and huddling under thornbushes (30:7), and (7) acting like fools who are so debased that they do not even deserve to be given names (30:8). Such vagabond rogues as met that description disdained Job as one lower than themselves. No wonder he was miserable! How humiliating and depressing that the scum of society should consider *him* as scum.

Their actions against Job included mockery (30:9; cf. 30:1), hatred and keeping their distance (30:10a), spitting on him (30:10b; cf. 17:6), lack of restraint ("bridle," [30:11b]), and attacking him, perhaps both physically and verbally (30:12-15). Their attacks were described in warfare imagery, like the attacks of an army against a city (cf. 19:12, where Job used similar wording). Their "brood"[26] rose against him, knocked him off his feet, built a siege ramp against him (cf. 19:12), broke up his path (i.e., made it impassable),[27] succeeded in destroying him without anyone's even helping them ("restrains" here means

26. This word, occurring only here in the Old Testament, seems to suggest contemptible offshoots (cf. Pope, p. 221).
27. The Hebrew word for "break up" is another word that occurs only here.

"helps"), ran at him like soldiers barging through a hole in a city wall, and rolled in[28] while the bricks of the wall were tumbling down around them. In such savage attacks, Job was overtaken by terror. His prestige was pursued (i.e., driven away) as if blown by the wind (cf. 19:9), and his prosperity vanished like a cloud. It is noteworthy that God along with the urchins is cited by Job as a cause for his troubles: "He has loosed His bowstring and afflicted me" (30:11). The image of God shooting him with an arrow recalls Job's earlier words (6:4; 16:12c, 13).

In the next section (30:16-23), Job voiced the agony of his physical and emotional pain from the hands of God. The pouring out of Job's soul upon him (30:16) expressed despondency (cf. Psalm 42:4) in the sense that his soul was drained of all zest for life.[29] He was in the grip of suffering for days on end, and at night his suffering was as intense as if swords had pierced to his very bones. (The bones were considered the place of acute pain [e.g., Psalm 42:10]). His gnawing pain was continuous.[30] "By a great force my garment is distorted" (30:18) is difficult to interpret for two reasons: the cause of the action is unclear (does the great force refer to Job's disease or to God?), and the meaning of the verb "distorted" is obscure. The thought may be (1) that his running sores had discolored and fouled his clothing, or (2) that his clothing was twisted by his agonized tossing and turning, or (3) that God grabbed him by the clothing and threw him down. Perhaps the first of these is to be preferred.

Verse 18b refers either to God's gripping Job tightly, as the collar of his robe gripped him, or to the disease's gripping him.

The "He" in 30:19 is no doubt God, and that fact may lend support to the view that God is the subject of 30:18 also. Job felt that God had humiliated him. Being "cast . . . into the mire" and becoming "like dust and ashes" refer to Job's hideous appearance or to his inner dejection. Possibly both thoughts were in-

28. A picturesque way of describing the waves of troops rushing in.
29. Pope, p. 222.
30. "Gnawing pains" renders the Hebrew word "gnawers," which means worms, or his urchin enemies (cf. "gnaw" in 30:3), or more likely, his pain.

131

tended. Job's cry to God for help was ignored (cf. 19:7), and his effort to get God's attention by standing up (meaning either in court or in a persistent attitude) was also useless (30:20). Not only was God passively indifferent; He also was actively cruel, pursuing Job like a ferocious beast (30:21) and like a terrible storm tossing him helplessly in the wind and causing him to melt in fear (30:22; cf. 27:21-22). God, who had thrown him into the mud, now tossed him in the wind. In despair, Job sensed that God would eventually end his life in death. "The house of meeting for all living" (30:23) to which God would bring him means death, the appointed place where all the living eventually meet. This is one of many times that Job despaired of life and spoke of death (3:20-23; 7:21; 10:20-22; 14:13-14; 16:22; 17:16; 19:26-27; 21:23, 26; 24:19, 24).

Having said that in his physical and emotional pain he was neglected by God (30:16-23), the patriarchal sufferer then bemoaned that in his agonizing pain he had been neglected by man too (30:24-31). It is natural for a person to cry for help when in disaster (30:24), Job explained. And yet his plight was so undeserved. He had been intensely concerned for others, weeping and grieving for those in need (30:25; cf. 29:12-16). Certainly he should receive the same kind of compassionate concern, but instead of good, he received evil, and instead of light, darkness (30:26). His trio of comforters had failed to do for him what he had done for others. Then Job elaborated on his condition: Inwardly he was in an emotional turmoil (literally, "my inward parts are boiling"), he was unable to relax, and only affliction confronted him day after day (30:27; cf. 30:16).

The word "mourning" (30:28) means "to be dark or blackened," suggesting here either that he was gloomy emotionally[31] or that his skin was dark from the disease.[32] "Without comfort" is literally "without heat," suggesting that his gloomy disposition (or his dark skin) was not from the heat of the sun. Again Job said that he stood and cried for help (cf. 30:20)—in such mournful tones that he sounded like the jackal with its doleful howl (cf. Mic 1:8) or the ostrich with its weird groans (cf. Isa 13:21; 34:

31. Pope, p. 224.
32. Reichert, p. 156.

13). Symptoms of his disease are cited: the blackening of the skin, and the inner burning with fever (30:30). (The word "black" is not the Hebrew word that was rendered "mourning" [but means black] in 30:28, nor is the word "fever" [literally, heat] the same word as the one rendered "comfort" [but meaning heat] in 30:28.)

Job concluded his plaintive rehearsal of his present remorse by stating that his joy had turned to grief (30:31). His harp and flute, instruments for expressing joy (cf. 21:12), now played only funeral dirges in accompaniment to people weeping in grief. The last five verses alternate between emotional pain (30:27, 29, 31) and physical pain (30:28, 30). The urchins mocked, spit, and attacked; God remained silent; friends were unsympathetic; and Job groaned in pain. Such was the plight of Job—the former plutocrat.

e. *Job's declaration of his innocence* (chap. 31). The memories of his past glory (chap. 29) followed by the painful recital of his present miseries (chap. 30) are followed logically by an oath of innocence (chap. 31) designed to demonstrate that the miseries of the present are undeserved. Not stated arrogantly, these words constitute Job's final effort to extricate himself from the false accusations made by his assailants and from his injustices at God's hand. The negative confession, in which the accused wished on himself a curse if he were guilty of the charges, was a strong form of denial of guilt. "If Job were innocent God's continued silence would clear his name and vindicate his integrity. If Job had sworn falsely God would be forced to intervene and impose the [punishment] Job had designated."[33]

In two ways, Job affirmed his ethical purity: (1) by recalling his previously made covenant, which was ethically binding (31:1), and (2) by using the "if guilty" oath ("if" occurs in 31:5, 7, 9, 13, 16, 19, 20 [twice], 21, 24, 25, 26, 38, 39) sometimes followed by the imprecation "let" (31:6, 8, 10, 22, 40) and sometimes not.[34]

---

33. Norman C. Habel, *The Book of Job* (New York: Cambridge U., 1975), p. 164.
34. The questions introduced by "Have" in 31:29, 31, 33 actually are statements that begin with "If" in the Hebrew and are not followed by imprecation. Thus they may be translated as questions or as statements.

Job cited his attitudes as well as his actions, the inner motives behind his outer conduct. Those attitudes thus revealed that his actions were nonhypocritical. Not only was he innocent of adultery (31:9-12); he was not even guilty of the lustful look (31:1). He had not acquired wealth unfairly (31:5-8), nor had he even trusted in riches (31:24-25). In addition to never cursing an enemy (31:30), he did not even rejoice in the downfall of an enemy (31:29).

The crimes enumerated in chapter 31 are ethical in nature and "are not, for the most part, monstrous crimes but minute deviations from the loftiest standards of ethics and piety."[35] Job had set the stage for this chapter earlier (23:11-12; 27:2-6). Rather than cite *only* public wrongs for which he might have been legally culpable[36] (such as the allegations Eliphaz had made pertaining to aggressive malignity against kinsmen, and Job's obdurate refusal to help the weary and hungry people, widows, and orphans [22:6-9]), Job delved to the deeper levels of the human conscience. Because purity was there, he implied, certainly he was unimpeachable in actions stemming from those motives.

The chapter may be divided into three sections: (1) Job had no secret sensual desires or dishonesty before men (31:1-12), (2) Job had not abused his power toward his slaves, the poor, or the helpless (31:13-23), (3) Job had shown no dishonesty or unfairness toward God or man (31:24-40).

Lust was denied by Job in 31:1-4. He had made a covenant with his eyes, and therefore was committed to avoiding lustful looks at girls. Knowing that the look could lead to desire in the heart, which desire could lead to sinful action, Job had resolved that he would avoid the very source of potential sin (cf. Prov 6:25; Matt 5:28). Job knew that the portion, or heritage (i.e., judgment), that comes from God on the one who sins (31:2) is calamity and disaster (31:3). (In 31:2, Job used words similar to Zophar's final statement in 20:29 and to his own words

35. Matitiahu Tsevat, "The Meaning of the Book of Job," *Hebrew Union College Annual* 77 (1966):38.
36. Georg Fohrer, "The Righteous Man in Job 31," in *Essays in Old Testament Ethics,* ed. James C. Crenshaw and John T. Willis (New York: KTAV Publishing, 1974), p. 13.

in 27:13.) Does not God, who "sees everything under the heavens" (28:24), "see my ways, and number all my steps?" asked Job (31:4). The question suggested the answer: God saw all Job's actions and would also know his thoughts. Therefore, Job implied, God could have struck him dead long ago if he had been guilty of breaking his covenant. Job had previously accused God of watching him constantly (7:19-20; 13:27). Now Job turned that action of God to his own advantage: God, who sees and knows his actions, would know that he was innocent.

Falsehood was denied by Job (31:5-8). Not only were his eyes innocent of lustful looks, but his feet were inculpable too. That is, he had not walked with falsehood as if it were a companion, nor had he pursued after deceit. That is a figurative way of saying that he has had nothing to do with deception. His integrity (the same word used earlier [2:3, 9]) would be evident to God if He were to weigh Job's heart against God's standards (31:6). If he had turned from the way (i.e., God's path of righteousness [cf. 23:11]), or if he had desired what he saw (cf. 31:1), or if he had even one blemish on his hands as evidence of wrongdoing (31:7), he was willing that he not enjoy the results of his work invested in farming.

Adultery was denied in strong words (31:9-12). The penalty invoked in this oath matched the crime: If Job had given in to the enticements of a woman (cf. 31:1) and had himself waited for an opportunity to have illicit relations with his neighbor's wife, he was willing that his wife become a slave for someone else (the grinding of corn by hand with millstones was a menial task of female slaves [Exod 11:5]) and be degraded sexually by others (31:9-10). This imprecation demonstrates Job's firm convictions regarding his innocence, for no man would readily subject his wife to such a terrible curse (Deut 28:30). Adultery was considered a disgustingly lewd crime, punishable by man in court. In addition, the sin itself brought its own punishment: Like a fire consuming a man to the very point of destruction in death (suggested by the word "Abaddon," a synonym of *Sheol* [cf. 26:6; 28:22]), it consumes a man's soul, destroying his reputation, his

135

conscience, his body, his family relationships, his future, and even his increase (i.e., crops as a source of income) (31:11-12).

Job next turned to another subject, his humane treatment of his slaves (31:13-15) and of the needy (31:16-23). He was not guilty of the oppression of his "very many servants" (1:3) or of hardheartedness toward the poor, widows, or orphans. With his wealth and power, he could have wronged his servants, but he denied any such abuse. Job's slaves, although his property, could bring complaints against him, and he did not refuse to hear them as some potentates may have ruthlessly done. He gave two reasons for his unusual attention to the grievances and requests of his slaves: he was answerable to God as his Judge (31:14), and both he and his slaves were made by the same God in the womb (31:15). Job's words are a lofty statement about the equality of the human race. Although people live in different social strata, in God's sight all are subject alike to His judging after they die and all are fashioned alike by His creative work before they are born. Job had spoken eloquently about God's concern in fashioning him intricately in the womb (10:8-11); now Job acknowledged that the same detailed care had been shown to his servants.

Concern for the poor, widows, orphans, and the needy (31:16-21) had been the reason God had blessed Job in the past (29:12-17). Earlier, Eliphaz had falsely accused Job of failing to help those in need (22:7-9), and Job had briefly and indirectly responded to that charge by pointing out that the wicked, not Job, were involved in such misconduct (24:9-10). In his oath (31:16-21), Job specifically repudiated those false allegations. He did not refuse to give the poor what they asked for, nor did he disappoint the expectations of widows, selfishly eat his food alone without sharing it with orphans, fail to give orphans fatherly care and guide widows, allow anyone to die from lack of clothing or coverings, fail to warm anyone with fleece from his sheep, or mistreat the orphans, thinking that other judges in the court would support him (the meaning of "support in the gate," the place of court proceedings) in his verdict against the weak.

The imprecation follows Job's last point (31:21). If he had

lifted up his hand (i.e., taken advantage of his rank to oppress an orphan), Job was willing that his shoulder fall off and his arm be broken at the elbow (31:22). Being terrified by God's ability to destroy wrongdoers was a deterrent against wrongdoing; and an awareness of God's majesty restrained Job from committing sin (31:23). Although his money and rank might have allowed him to influence judges and neglect the needy without his being punished, his prominence would be useless in forestalling the judgment of God.

Job then disclaimed any involvement in materialism (31:24-25), idolatry (31:26-28), revenge (31:29-30), miserliness (31:31-32), hypocrisy (31:33-34), or exploitation (31:38-40). His denial of trusting in his gold (31:24) answered Eliphaz's implied accusation (22:24). Nor did he pride himself in his wealth (31:25). An idolatrous worship of nature was denied. Job had never allowed himself to be enticed with a worshipful look at the sun or moon (31:26) or a worshipful act toward them, such as kissing the hand and extending it to the two major heavenly bodies as a gesture of adoration and gratitude.[37] Worship of these objects in the sky was common in the ancient Near East. For Job to have participated in such nature worship would have been a denial of the Creator and thus would have resulted in judgment (31:28). It is noteworthy that this is the fifth time that Job mentioned God in the chapter (31:2-4, 6, 14-15, 23, 28). Without question Job was aware of God's omniscience, judgment, creative power, majesty, and existence.

Not only had Job never adored the sky's two major luminaries by kissing his hand with his mouth, but also he had not allowed his mouth to sin by cursing an enemy. In fact, he had not even secretly been glad when an enemy died or faced trouble (31:29-30; cf. Prov 17:5b; 24:17). Here, as before (31:24-27), there was neither the inner attitude nor the outer action.

The absence of miserliness on Job's part was indicated by "the men of [his] tent" (meaning his family members, servants, or, more probably, travelers lodging overnight), who spoke of his

37. Idols were kissed (1 Kings 19:18; Hos 13:2), but because the sun and the moon could not be reached, the hand was kissed and extended to the revered objects.

universal generosity with his food (31:31).[38] Job added that he continually took in the stranger and traveler, thus offering both food and lodging (31:32).

Hypocrisy was another sin Job denied (31:33-34). He had not covered his rebellion, as Adam had attempted to do (Gen 3:7-10), or attempted to hide his iniquity in his bosom. Some commentators and Bible versions render "like Adam" with the words "like man," which is a possible rendering of the Hebrew, but Job's statement would have had more impact if he had referred to Adam's hiding. Was Job admitting here that he was guilty of sin, after all? Not necessarily. Instead, he was stating that *if* he had been conscious of sin, he would have made no effort to hide it as if it did not exist. His reason for not being hypocritical—if he had had any sins to hide—was that the public would have scorned him, thus making it necessary for him to keep silent (rather than try to justify himself) and stay inside. Such a prominent person could not be hypocritical for long; people would know his sins and would scorn him.

In 31:35-37, Job made a final effort to have God answer his arguments. He longed for someone to hear him: "Oh that I had one to hear me!" Because of Job's earlier statement (30:20), this cry probably refers to his desire for God to listen. Job figuratively attached his signature to his oath of purity ("Behold, here is my signature") and then asked that God respond to the oath ("Let the Almighty answer me!") either with the punishments cited in his self-imprecations or with vindication. Job was so certain of his innocence of motive and action that he would proudly carry the indictment of God, whom he called his adversary (literally, man of my indictment; cf. 13:24; 16:9; 19:11, where different words for adversary are used), on his shoulder and wear it as a crown.[39] Job would proudly exhibit such a citation of trumped-up charges, because in his innocence he could confidently refute all God's incriminations. He would readily give an account to God of the way he had walked (31:37a; cf.

38. It is not necessary to see in this phrase a reference to safety from homosexual abuse as Habel (p. 167) and Pope (pp. 236-37) do.
39. Habel understands the legal document (literally, scroll) to be Job's verdict of acquittal written by God (pp. 168-69), but the context seems to indicate a list of charges or allegations.

138

31:4), concealing nothing; and in princely confidence he would approach Him (31:37b), waiting for God's verdict of acquittal.

Although many scholars feel that 31:38-40 is out of place and should be inserted elsewhere in the chapter, the verses may be an example of an anticlimactic passage at the end of a chapter, creating a trailing-off effect (cf., e.g., 19:28-29). Job's land would protest to God against him either as a witness to the alleged wrongs cited earlier in the chapter, or more likely, out of concern for the fraud or injustice done by Job when he had cultivated the land. (Examples of such fraud or injustice would be forcing others to work for him, imposing unreasonable demands, or paying inadequate wages.)[40] The furrows also were personified as weeping because of the injustice to its workers. If he had "eaten its fruit without money" (i.e., eaten the produce of the land without paying its workers) or had caused its workers ("owners" may be understood as "workers") to die from hard work or starvation, Job wished that the land would become totally worthless to him. Wishing that the land be overrun with briars instead of wheat or with stinkweed instead of barley, if he were guilty of injustice to the land, is another imprecation that matched the offense. Stronger than the uprooting of crops mentioned earlier (31:8), it means that the land would become utterly useless for any further crops. And with that word of certitude, Job's words of argumentation with his talkative friends and of self-justice before a silent God were ended. Job rested his case; the next move was God's.

40. Barnes, 2:116.

11

The Angry Young Man

E. ELIHU'S FOUR SPEECHES (chaps. 32—37)

The long, almost monotonous debate between Job and his comrades had ended. Although persistent in their view that suffering is retributive, the ash-heap trio were eventually silenced by Job's stronger insistence that he was undeserving of such calamities. Because their repeated efforts could not budge him from what they considered a self-righteous attitude, they gave up (32:1).

Although Job could reduce them *to* silence, he could not induce God *out* of silence! Job persisted in his demand for vindication from God; he hoped that that vindication would demonstrate that God was acting out of character and should therefore withdraw his suffering.

Deeply angered by both sides of the debate he had been listening to, a fifth person then entered the discussion. Many commentators assume that Elihu's four speeches (chaps. 32—37) were added to the book sometime after the original version had been written.[1] It is argued, for example, that he is not mentioned elsewhere in the book. When God condemned the friends and commended Job (chap. 42), Elihu was ignored; thus it can be suggested that he was not part of the story. But is it not possible that Elihu was closer to the truth and therefore not to be included with the three friends, about whom God said, "[They] have not

---

1. Freedman, however, suggests the novel view that Elihu's first speech (32:6—33:33) belongs after chapter 14, the second speech (chap. 34) should follow chapter 27, the third speech (chap. 35) may follow chapter 21, and the fourth speech (chaps. 36-37) should go after chapter 31—each speech following words spoken by Job (David N. Freedman, "The Elihu Speeches in the Book of Job," *Harvard Theological Review* 61 [1968]:51-59). But this conjectural hypothesis would disrupt the pattern of the cycle of speeches and fails to account for 32:1-6, which states that Elihu waited till the three friends had ended their speeches.

spoken of Me what is right" (42:7)? In the end, God did not answer Satan or Job's wife; therefore, was he obligated to answer Elihu? The absence of reference to Elihu in the prologue is understandable, for he was a younger listener and was not involved in the rounds of debate.

Differences in style and language are cited as proof that the Elihu speeches were a later addition.[2] Elihu addressed Job by name and quoted Job directly, whereas the three friends did not do so; and he used "El" for God and used a number of Aramaic words more than the three counselors did. However, those stylistic differences simply point up his distinctive character.[3]

The argument that Elihu makes no contribution to the book is readily answered by the observation that his view of suffering is distinct from that of the three friends and that his view of God is higher than theirs. In addition, he made an honest effort to provide answers to Job's complaints about God rather than repeat the you-have-what-you-deserve view of the other three. Whereas Elihu's three elders had recommended that Job repent of willful sin committed prior to his calamities, Elihu recommended (1) that Job repent of pride that developed because of the suffering, and (2) that Job exalt God's work (36:24), consider His works (37:14), and fear Him (37:24). The three counselors had claimed that Job was suffering because he was sinning, but Elihu explained that he was sinning because he was suffering! His suffering led him to an attitude of pride before God and a questioning of God's ways. The triad diagnosis pertained to sinful actions in Job's past experience, whereas Elihu's diagnosis dealt with sinful attitudes in Job's present life.

Although Job did not answer Elihu (which silence is used in the argument that Elihu's speeches were inserted later), Elihu's final words seem to prepare the scene for God's breakthrough (chaps. 38—41). In addition, Elihu's words may have silenced Job, which silence the three friends were unable to produce; or Elihu may simply not have prodded Job to respond.

2. E.g., S. R. Driver and G. B. Gray, *A Critical and Exegetical Commentary on the Book of Job*, pp. xl-xlix.
3. E. Dhorme, *A Commentary on the Book of Job*, p. ciii; and Francis I. Andersen, *Job: An Introduction and Commentary*, p. 52.

Thus considered, the Elihu section provides a smooth transition from Job's proud insistence for vindication (chap. 31) to God's communication. Why should God be expected to reply to Job immediately after Job's words were ended? After all, God had previously not replied to Job's demands for a hearing in court with God (13:3, 15; 16:21; 30:20).[4]

1. *Introduction to Elihu* (32:1-5)

The poetry section of the book (3:1—42:6) is broken in one place by prose (32:1-6a), which is necessary in order to introduce Elihu, a fourth protagonist. After the smoke of the verbal skirmishes between the three and the one had cleared (32:1), Elihu felt free to speak. His genealogy is longer than that of any other character in the book. As a Buzite, he was related to Abraham, for Buz was a brother of Uz and a son of Nahor, who was Abraham's brother (Gen 22:20-21). Buz, Tema, and Dedan are Arab locations (Jer 25:23). "Of the family of Ram" suggests that Elihu was an ancestor of David (Ruth 4:19-22).

Elihu's anger, pent up while he was waiting in deference to his elders (32:4), was intense. Four times in this section it is said that his "anger burned." That anger was in two directions: toward Job for seeking to justify himself before God (32:2),[5] and toward the three counselors because they had pronounced him guilty without adequate proof (32:3). He seemed to burst in as if he had an answer to the wrongs on both sides and a solution to the impassse. The companions of Job are twice called the "three men" rather than the "three friends" (32:1, 5).

The wordiness of this introduction matches Elihu's pompous style.[6]

2. *Elihu's first speech* (32:6—33:33)

a. *Elihu's self-introduction* (32:6-22). Elihu's first speech to Job really begins in 33:1; it is preceded by a lengthy justification of his own speaking, which justification includes his respect for the three counselors (32:6-10), his evaluation of them (32:

---

4. T. Miles Bennett, *When Human Wisdom Fails: An Exposition of the Book of Job* (Grand Rapids: Baker, 1971), p. 78.
5. The Hebrew could mean that Job considered himself right and God wrong.
6. H. H. Rowley, *Job*, p. 264.

11-14), and his desire to speak (32:15-22). Because of his younger age, he was shy and fearful to give opinion (32:6), thinking that older persons are wiser (32:7). But then he said that he realized that wisdom[7] comes from God, not from years ("a spirit in man" and "the breath of the Almighty" may refer to the Spirit of God, which is often associated with wisdom[8] [Gen 41:38-39; Exod 31:3; Num 27:18-21; Isa 11:2; Dan 5:11-12]). In view of his daring assertion that his elders were ignorant, he found it necessary to plead for a hearing. ("Listen to me" and "let me speak" are repeated by Elihu numerous times [32:10, 20; 33:1, 12, 31, 33; 34:2, 10, 16; 37:14].)

Elihu waited, listening closely to their arguments, and concluded that they were unable to refute Job (32:11-12). Job had said that man cannot find wisdom (chap. 28), and therefore they should not claim to have it or conclude that because they could not refute Job, God would (32:13). Another way to understand that verse is to take the last line, "God will rout him, not man," as Elihu's words rather than the words of the three friends. In that case, the thought is that man's wisdom cannot defeat Job's arguments; only God can do that. Therefore, Elihu would not argue as the three friends had done (32:14), but rather with the wisdom of God. If that is the proper interpretation, then Elihu was saying that they were without God's wisdom, but that he had it.

Having spoken to the three counselors (32:6-14), Elihu then turned and spoke to Job (32:15-22). Because the three counselors were dismayed and had nothing more to say, Elihu would no longer wait. He would tell his opinion (32:15-17). The two lines in 32:17 each begin with the Hebrew words for "even I," thus hinting again at his modesty in view of his younger age. Regarding his statement, "I am full of words" (32:18a), Rowley humorously comments, "none would dispute this."[9] He was con-

---

7. In his speeches, Elihu referred to wisdom eleven times, using four different words.
8. Marvin E. Tate, "The Speeches of Elihu," *Review and Expositor* 68 (Fall 1971):491.
9. Rowley, p. 267. There is no question that Elihu was wordy, for the verses of his speeches total 156, longer than Job's final speech of 148 verses and longer than all the speeches of any one of the friends (cf. Eliphaz's 110 verses, Bildad's 46, and Zophar's 47).

strained to speak ("the spirit within me" [32:18*b*] may be his inner spirit, not the Spirit of God, in view of the following two verses). His pent-up constraint was compared to fermenting wine about to cause even new wineskins (without a hole for venting) to burst (32:19). He then requested relief from his bottled condition, determining not to be partial to Job, the friends, or God (Job had accused the three of showing partiality toward God in disfavor toward Job [13:8, 10]) or to use flattery, for fear of God's vengeance (32:20-22). In summary, Elihu's five self-assigned qualifications for speaking were: The Spirit of God was in him, he had waited for the three counselors to finish, he had different and better arguments, he had a lot to say, and he was impartial and nonflattering. His anger had not caused him to lose his sense of self-importance.

b. *Elihu's first answer to Job* (chap. 33). In the first of Elihu's four speeches, he refuted Job's charges that God did not hear him (chap. 33). In his second speech, he refuted Job's charge that God is unjust (chap. 34). And in his third speech, he refuted Job's charge that it is useless to serve God (chap. 35). He discussed God's communications to man (through dreams and pain) (chap. 33); he commented on God's justice with man (chap. 34); and he discussed God's sovereignty over man (chap. 35). Then in the final speech (chaps. 36—37), he again elaborated on God's justice and sovereignty.

Elihu's first speech (chap. 33) opens with Elihu requesting that Job listen (33:1-7). Elihu was garrulously redundant (33:1-2), but his sincerity (33:3) was evident by virtue of the fact that he was created by God's Spirit and given life by the breath of the Almighty (33:4), and his certainty (33:5) was evident by his challenge to Job[10] to refute him by arraying himself in battle poise against Elihu. The young, angry man considered himself to be equal with Job before God (and not superior to him, as had the friends), for both were God's possessions and creations, formed (literally, nipped) out of clay (cf. 31:15). Therefore, because they were equals, Elihu would not terrify

---

10. "Yourselves" (33:5) should be "yourself." Elihu is addressing Job, not the three friends.

him (as Job had frequently said God had done to him [7:14; 9:34; 13:21; 23:15]), nor would he pressure him (33:6-7).

In the next six verses (33:8-13), Elihu summarized what he had heard Job say (33:8) in his charges against God: (1) Job claimed to be innocent ("I am pure,[11] without transgression;[12] I am innocent and there is no guilt in me"[13] [33:9])—answered (chap. 35) by the fact that God is sovereign and therefore is unaffected by man's guilt or innocence; (2) Job claimed that God treated him unjustly ("Behold, He invents pretexts[14] against me; He counts me as His enemy.[15] He puts my feet in the stocks;[16] He watches all my paths"[17] [33:10-11])—answered (chap. 34) by the fact that God is just; and (3) Job claimed that God ignored his pleas and did not listen to him ("Why do you complain[18] against Him, that He does not give an account of all His doings?" [33:13])—answered (chap. 33) by the fact that God is communicative.

In chapter 33 Elihu was answering Job's question, "Why doesn't God respond to me?" In chapter 34 the question he was answering was "Why doesn't God relieve me [from my unjust suffering]?" And in chapter 35, Elihu discussed Job's question, "Why doesn't He reward me [for my innocence]?"

Elihu did not hesitate to be blunt with Job, telling him "you are not right in this, for God is greater than man" (33:12).

Elihu's refutation of Job's view that God does not respond was frontal: God *does* speak, and He does so in dreams (33:14-18) and through sickness and pain (33:19-28). Whereas God does not report to man on His actions, He does communicate with him: "Indeed God speaks once, or twice [i.e., in various ways, or with repetition], yet no one notices it" (33:14).[19] God had spo-

11. Cf. 6:10; 9:21; 10:7; 13:18; 16:17.
12. Cf. 7:20-21; 13:23; 14:17; 23:11.
13. Cf. 9:20; 10:7; 14; 27:6.
14. The Hebrew word is "occasions," which means pretexts for hostility (Victor E. Reichert, *Job*, p. 171). God, according to Job, had to make up reasons for punishing him, for there was no basis for it in Job's character.
15. Cf. 13:24; 19:11.
16. Cf. 13:27.
17. Cf. 7:17-20; 13:27.
18. "Complain" means "present an indictment," a legal term Job had used several times.
19. Here Elihu said that God speaks "once, or twice," and in 33:29 (marg.) Elihu said that God speaks "twice, three times."

ken more than once to Job, Elihu contended, but Job had not been listening. Elihu spoke of "men" and "man" (33:14-30), thus indirectly including Job.

Eliphaz, the senior legate, had begun his attack on Job by referring to a spooky dream in which God allegedly had revealed to him the fact of man's impurity (4:12-21). That dream had been the basis of Eliphaz's authority over Job. Elihu, on the other hand, referred to dreams as God's way of instructing man and keeping him from sin. When God "opens the ears of men" (33:16a), He gets their attention. And when God "seals their instruction" (33:16b), He "communicates warnings to men on their beds, in a manner as solemn and impressive as if it were ratified with a seal, and made as secure as possible."[20] The purpose of God's dream-communications, Elihu purported, was to turn man from wrong deeds and the wrong attitude of pride (33:17). The word "conduct" is the word for "deed," which frequently has an evil connotation (e.g., Gen 44:15; Exod 23:24; Neh 6:14; Eccles 4:3; 8:11; Mic 6:16; etc.). The words "keep man from pride" are literally "cover pride from man." Evil actions and sinful pride lead to death (33:18), but God keeps man's soul from the pit (used five times in this chapter [33:18, 22, 24, 28, 30], each time meaning the grave) and from "perishing by the sword" (a reading preferred to "passing over into Sheol").[21] Being frightened by nightmares (7:14), Job missed the purpose of God's dream-warnings, namely, to preserve man from sin and death.

A second way God speaks to man, according to Elihu, is through sickness (33:19-28). Physical pain, felt inwardly to his very bones, causes him to lose his appetite (33:19-20), which results in his losing weight so that his bones protrude (33:21). Elihu obviously had Job in mind, for Job had said that he hated

---

20. Albert Barnes, *Notes, Critical, Illustrative, and Practical, on the Book of Job,* 2:132.
21. Some scholars suggest the rendering "kept from crossing the channel," meaning the "river of death," according to Akkadian parallels (e.g., Marvin H. Pope, *Job,* p. 250). However, "sword" is the normal meaning of the Hebrew word ("perish by the sword" is used later by Elihu [36:12]). Death by the sword certainly is fitting in the context, which speaks of death.

food (6:7). Such illness, Elihu continued, brings a man close to death (33:22).[22]

In dreams, God can give instructions that will divert a man's soul from sin and consequential death. Likewise, in sickness (both are bed experiences, certainly known to Job), God can send an angel as a mediator-interpreter between God and man "to remind a man what is right for him" (33:23). Here Elihu contradicted Eliphaz, who had stated earlier that no angels could assist Job in his plight (5:1). Job too had bemoaned the absence of an arbiter to intercede on his behalf (9:33).

The instruction from dreams is negative, whereas that from angels in times of sickness is positive. The angel's being "one out of a thousand" indicates that God has numerous angels to minister to and instruct His saints. By reminding man of what is right for him, the angel leads him back to uprightness, which he enjoyed before his sickness—which was perhaps caused by sin. "Then let him be gracious to him" (33:24a) can be rendered "he is gracious to him," the "he" referring either to God or, more likely, to the angel, who asks God to "deliver him from going down to the pit," because he (the angel) has "found a ransom" (33:24b).

Whether the unspecified ransom is the repentance of the sick person or a gracious atonement provided by the angel, the result is restoration to vigorous health (33:25),[23] and spiritual renewal (33:26-28). The latter includes prayer, acceptance by God, joy in God's presence (which is amazingly similar to Eliphaz's words [22:26]), a righteous standing before God, a singing testimony to men, and verbal testimony before men. A better translation of "it is not proper for me" (33:27) is "it did not agree with me." The verb "agree" is literally "be even or level," and from that literal meaning comes the idea of being equal to or of the same value as. The thought here is that the restored sinner will realize that his sin did not give him any advantage and instead worked

22. "His life [draws near] to those who bring death" may refer to angels who bring death, as in Psalm 78:49. If so, this implied reference to angels subtly leads to the reference to the angel in the next verse, Job 33:23.

23. "Let his flesh become" and "let him return" (33:25) can be translated "his flesh will become" and "he will return."

against him, for it brought him only sickness. "Redeemed" (33: 28) is from the same root as "deliver" (33:24). Because the sick man has been redeemed through the intervening work of an angel, he has been delivered from death ("pit" [33:28] is used for the fourth time in this chapter; each time it means "death"). In addition, his "life shall see the light," meaning he shall be alive.

Elihu then summarized the two purposes of God in dreams and sickness, which he brings repeatedly (literally, "twice, three times"): negatively, to keep man from death, and positively, to give him a satisfying life (33:29-30). To be "enlightened with the light of life" is one of the frequent Old Testament occasions of equating being alive with seeing the light (or being in the light). This obviously contrasts with the darkness of the grave. Elihu then pleaded with Job to listen attentively for two reasons: he desired to justify Job, and he had wisdom to share (33:31-33).

Elihu viewed suffering as protective, rather than retributive, as a means of keeping man from death rather than as a means of punishment leading him to death. The three companions had stressed suffering's punitive value, whereas Elihu underscored its pedagogical value. (However, it should be noted that Eliphaz also touched briefly on the disciplinary benefit of suffering [5: 17]). To the three counselors, sickness was the punishment of a judge for sins committed; but for Elihu, illness was God's way of getting man's attention, reminding him of what is right, atoning for his sin, and diverting him away from sin. To Elihu as well as the three older men, sin was behind the suffering. But Elihu's solution was not "repent of your sin and God will restore you," but "listen to an angel, who will provide a reminder and redemption, and God will restore you." For the friends, the restoration depended on man's initiative; for Elihu it depended on God's initiative through an angel.

Who was correct—Elihu or the three friends? Other passages of Scripture reveal that God uses suffering for either purpose, sometimes as judgment of sin and at other times as prevention from death. Although Elihu was nearer the truth, both he and the three counselors were wrong, because they presupposed that Job had sinned prior to his suffering. Furthermore, when God spoke to Job (chaps. 38—41), He did so directly, rather than through an angel, as Elihu had proposed, and nothing was said about redemption.[24] Elihu, however, was correct in touching on pride, which had become Job's problem as a result of his suffering, and he was probably correct in his discussion of the purpose of dreams in Job's situation.

3. *Elihu's second speech* (chap. 34)

In his second speech, Elihu proceeded to answer Job's accusation that God was unjust. The young protagonist spoke first to the three friends (34:1-15), as indicated by the plural "you" and references to "wise men" (34:2) and "men of understanding" (34:10).[25] He then spoke directly to Job (34:16-37), as indicated by the singular "you."

a. *Quotation of Job* (34:1-9). Elihu again requested his elders to listen to him, to examine what he would say,[26] and to decide whether Job was right or wrong in accusing God of unrighteousness in defense of his own righteousness (34:2-4). He then quoted Job indirectly—"I am righteous" (34:5*a*; cf. 13:18; 27:6) and "I am without transgression" (34:6*b*; cf. 13:23; 14:17; 23:11)—and directly—"God has taken away my [legal] right" (34:5*b*; cf. 27:2). Elihu also quoted Job as having asked, "Should I lie concerning my [legal] right?" (34:6*a*).[27]

Elihu then sided with the three counselors by speaking of Job as one "who drinks up derision like water" (a quotation of Eliphaz [15:16], though with a slight change and with more directness) and by charging that Job was a companion of wicked men (34:7-8). An additional indirect quotation of Job is given (34:9), perhaps recalling 9:30-31. This contention of Job's that de-

---

24. James F. Ross, "Job 33:14-30: The Phenomenology of Lament," *Journal of Biblical Literature* 94 (March 1975):42-43.
25. Elihu's reference to them as "wise men" may have been stated facetiously, for he had questioned their wisdom (32:6-9).
26. Job too had spoken about the ear testing words as the palate tastes food (12:11).
27. Some scholars render this "He [i.e., God] lied"; others translate it "Should I be considered a liar?"

lighting in God "profits a man nothing" is answered later by Elihu (chap. 35).

b. *Refutation of Job* (34:10-37). Elihu rose to the defense of God's justice, thus agreeing with the friends and accusing Job of insolence. It is unthinkable that the sovereign Creator-Ruler-Sustainer would be unjust. To do wickedness or wrong or to pervert justice would be contrary to God's nature (34:10, 12).[28] Elihu then proceeded to spell out the character of God as a means of demonstrating His justice: God is (1) the just Rewarder, giving man what he deserves (34:11); (2) the sovereign Authority, receiving His authority over the universe from no one and thus answerable to no one (34:13); (3) the independent Sustainer of life, having the power over the human race to continue man's life or to withdraw it at will (34:14-15); (4) the impartial Ruler, pronouncing kings to be worthless and nobles to be wicked, without any partiality to the influential or wealthy class, for all are His creation (34:16-20);[29] (5) the omniscient Judge, seeing all the steps of man, who cannot hide in darkness from Him, and knowing man and his actions immediately—without investigation in a court case[30] (34:21-25a); and (6) the absolute Executor, overthrowing the wicked at night (when they are not seen) or in a public place where they are seen (34:25b-30). The reason those mighty though wicked people are overthrown, Elihu maintained, is that they disobeyed and disregarded God by oppressing the poor, whose cries of anguish were heard by God (34:27-28). And yet, Elihu continued, if God "keeps quiet" or "hides His face" toward tyrants (i.e., if He does not act against injustice as soon as man thinks He should), man has no right to condemn God (34:29). Elihu obviously had in mind Job's condemning attitude. The place of the words, "That is, in

28. These words are mindful of Bildad's question, "Does God pervert justice or does the Almighty pervert what is right?" (8:3).

29. The point of 34:17 is that because an unjust human ruler is not tolerated by man, surely it is wrong to think of God, the "righteous mighty [O]ne," as being unjust. Elihu added that the wicked, even though they are mighty, are suddenly destroyed by God and often by surprise "at midnight" (34:20; cf. 34:25).

30. Verses 23-24 are strikingly similar to Zophar's statement, "For He knows false men, and He sees iniquity without investigating" (11:11). This is further evidence that Elihu sided with the three counselors in their defense of God's justice.

150

regard to both nation and man" (34:29c), in Elihu's thought is difficult to determine. One way of understanding it is to consider 34:29a-b as parenthetical so that the cry of the poor and afflicted (34:28) is heard by God, whether the afflicted is an entire nation or a single individual. At any rate, the result is that godless men are not allowed by God to rule or ensnare people interminably (34:30).

Having stated that God is answerable to no one (34:13), Elihu then applied that principle to Job (34:31-37). Someone may have the audacity to tell God that he has borne punishment[31] without having knowingly acted corruptly[32] and may therefore demand that God make known to him sins that were not evident to him ("what I do not see"),[33] with the assurance that he would not do it again—assuming he had sinned. Elihu then spoke directly to Job with the burning question, "Shall He recompense on your terms, because you have [objected]?" (34:33a). By this question, Elihu sought to show Job that God in His sovereignty is under no obligation to act as man thinks He should. Man's objecting to God's ways is no reason for God to change.

By telling Job that he must choose (34:33), Eilhu meant that it was up to Job, not Elihu, to suggest an alternative to God's ways of running the universe.[34] Elihu then indicated that men who are wise would condemn Job. (That was a clever way for Elihu to assert his wisdom, because he too was condemning Job.) They would accuse Job of speaking "without knowledge" and "without wisdom" (34:34-35); they would feel that he ought to be on trial "to the limit" (i.e., until he repented of such impudence against God), for he had spoken like wicked men (34:36; cf. 34:7-8). That cruel statement sounds like Zophar's cutting words that God was not giving him all the punishment he deserved (11:6). "Elihu's attitude matches that of Satan; hit a man hard enough and he will break."[35]

31. Although the word "punishment" ("chastisement") is not in the original, the thought is implied in the verb "borne."
32. "I did not act corruptly" more accurately renders the Hebrew of 34:31c.
33. Job had spoken in that vein to God (6:24; 10:2; 13:23).
34. Reichert, p. 180.
35. Norman C. Habel, *The Book of Job* (New York: Cambridge U., 1975), p. 186.

On top of the sin that brought on his suffering, Job was guilty of rebelling against God, asserted Elihu. Not only that, but Job clapped his hands in their presence; that is, he treated their counsel with contempt (clapping the hands was sometimes used to silence others),[36] and he "multiplie[d] his words against God."

Although Elihu had assured the three counselors that he would not use their kinds of arguments (32:14), he fell into the very trap they were in—claiming that the patriarch's belligerence evidenced wickedness—and he even used words almost identical to each of the three friends' words. Questioning God's ways was the height of earthly arrogance ("What man is like Job?" [34:7]). Because God "will not pervert justice" (34:12), Elihu reasoned, the only conclusion possible was that Job was in the wrong.

To what extent was Elihu correct? Certainly he was accurate in speaking of God's authority, sustenance and control of life, omniscience, power to judge sin, and sovereign privilege to be silent when He so chooses. Even Job had argued for those truths. And undoubtedly Elihu was right in reprimanding Job for his gall in demanding that God answer him (34:29) by showing him where he had sinned (34:32) and by recompensing on his terms (34:33). But like his three superiors, Elihu, in order to defend God, had to assume that Job was lying about his innocence. None of the five—Eliphaz, Bildad, Zophar, Elihu, and Job—knew of the contest in heaven between God and Satan. Consequently, Elihu's accusation was inaccurate. He failed to take into account the possibility that Job was suffering *without* due cause in specific sins. "The Bible recognizes that desert and fortune are not precisely matched. Any bland assurance that they are can never satisfy men of Job's honesty."[37]

4. *Elihu's third speech* (chap. 35)

In his third speech, Elihu rose to the defense of God's sovereignty in answer to Job's charge that God did not reward him for his innocence. His answer was twofold: (1) God is supreme, and thus He is not affected by or dependent on man's innocence

---

36. Or perhaps Elihu meant that Job clapped his hands in derision against God.
37. Rowley, p. 279.

or sin, and (2) God's lack of response to Job's cries was because of his pride.

a. *Quotation of Job* (35:1-3). Elihu's approach here was similar to that in the other chapters: He quoted Job (35:2-3) and then sought to refute him (35:4-16). Earlier, Elihu had quoted Job as having said that a righteous life seemingly does a person no good (34:9), recalling Job's words (9:30-31). Elihu now dealt with that posture of Job's. The young contender began by asking, "Do you think this is right? Do you say, 'My righteousness is [before God]'?"[38] (35:2). Although Job had not made that claim in so many words, his position was clear. Elihu's implication that Job was wrong in such a claim was quickly reinforced (35:3). How could you assert a righteous position before God when at the same time you asked what advantage there was to being innocent over being sinful?[39] Job had certainly questioned the value of serving God, for he had suffered with the wicked.

b. *Refutation of Job* (35:4-16). Elihu's youthful presumption was evident in his confidence to answer not only Job but also his friends (35:4).[40] By pointing Job to the heavens (the starry universe) and the clouds, which are "higher than you" (35:5), Elihu sought to remind Job that because they were greater than man, surely their Creator was greater than man. Because God is transcendent above the stars and clouds, He is not affected adversely by man's sin (35:6) or benefited by man's righteousness (35:7). Eliphaz had made a similar observation about the stars (22:12) and about God's indifference to man's conduct (22:2-3). A person's sin or his righteous living affects only man, not God (35:8). Elihu agreed with Eliphaz that man's actions do not influence God, but he carried that thought further and added that a person's character and conduct *do* influence himself and others.

Was Elihu suggesting that God is totally oblivious and indiffer-

---

38. "Before God" may be read instead of "more than God's."
39. The phrase "to You" (35:3) should read "to you," meaning Job rather than God.
40. "Friends" may refer to the three speakers or, as Ellison suggests, to the wicked, who, according to Elihu, were Job's companions (34:36; cf. 21:14-15) (H. L. Ellison, *A Study of Job: From Tragedy to Triumph,* p. 113).

ent to man? If so, his idea seems to contradict other parts of Scripture and also to conflict with what Elihu himself said in his next sentences (35:9-16, where the implication is clear that if God does not answer man because of his pride, He *does* answer man when he prays in humility).[41] Instead, Elihu was affirming that God's actions (of justice and benevolence) toward man are self-determined, not man-centered. God is not under man's control or subject to man's bribes (35:8). In other words, Elihu said that God's standards of justice are not flexible or partial. If He shows mercy, it is not because He has been induced by man's goodness; and if He inflicts judgment, it is not because He has been injured or fears man. Instead, Elihu said, both mercy and judgment are given because man deserves them.

Hence, because man will be judged by God's standards, there *is* an advantage to being holy rather than sinful.[42] Thus Elihu's argument was this: "Job, you reasoned that because you are suffering as the wicked do, there is no point to your being righteous. But there is an advantage to holy living. God does judge impartially and does not alter His standards by what man does or does not do. Your wickedness or righteousness may influence or bribe others, but not the sovereign God."

The second argument postulated by Elihu pertained to the reason God does not answer the prayers of the oppressed (35:9-16). Job had previously expressed concern over this problem (24:12; cf. 36:13), and Elihu had also referred to "the cry of the poor" because of unfair treatment by the mighty "workers of iniquity" (34:22-28). Their cry for help under oppression, Elihu explained, was only a cry for deliverance and was not a prayer to God in true humility. They did not turn to God as their Maker, recognizing Him as the one who can give "songs in the night" (i.e., joy in the time of trouble) and who can teach them more than the irrational animals and birds (35:10-11). The latter point is presumably Elihu's way of saying that the op-

41. Andersen seems to accept the view that this is what Elihu was saying and that Elihu thus "finished up in a corner" and was "saying in effect that justice means nothing to God" (Anderson, p. 256).

42. This view, expounded by Barnes (2:157-59), avoids making Elihu contradict himself and avoids making Elihu agree with Job that righteous living is useless.

pressed did not turn to God to learn from Him the reason for suffering. Because the animal kingdom is unable to gain any knowledge about the purpose of suffering, and because the oppressed did not ask God for instruction on the subject, the oppressed are like animals.

The attitude behind their cry was one of pride (35:12). Elihu's statement (35:12) was intended specifically for Job. Such cries, Elihu said, are not answered, listened to, or regarded by God, because they are empty, that is, devoid of the substance of sincerity (35:12-13).

Elihu said that if such insincere, proud prayers were not answered by God, certainly Job's cries of arrogance and impatience would not be heard (35:14). When Elihu said, "you say you do not behold Him," he was referring to Job's complaint that he could not find or see God (9:11; 23:8-9). Therefore, Elihu advised Job to wait for God because he had presented his case to Him (35:14b). "Job's problem had been with the hiddenness of God. Elihu counters by contending that Job will get his just deserts in due time."[43] Also, Elihu contended, Job supposed that God's unresponsiveness meant that He was indifferent to transgression[44] and consequently that Job was speaking emptily (i.e., with hollow, meaningless words) against God, multiplying words without knowledge (35:15-16; cf. 34:35, 37).

5. *Elihu's fourth speech* (chaps. 36—37)

Many Bible students agree that Elihu's final discourse contains his most impressive speech. He touched on the subjects seen in his first three speeches—suffering, God's justice, and God's sovereignty—but here he was on a loftier plane; the grandeur of his thoughts and the eloquence of his words were an octave higher than they had been in his previous orations. New dimensions of God's character were added. In addition to speaking of God's justice, Elihu also referred to His power; and in addition to his comments on God's sovereignty, Elihu spoke of God's benevolence.

43. Habel, p. 189.
44. This word, which occurs only here in the Old Testament, may be translated "folly."

155

The speech falls into two parts: God's justice and power in His dealings with man, both the wicked and the afflicted (36:1-25), and God's sovereignty and benevolence in His dealings with nature (36:26—37:24). All these verses are addressed to Job except 37:2-13, which are spoken to the three counselors (and, perhaps, to Job also) because of the plural "you" (37:2). In each section, after Elihu spoke of God's nature and works, he gave several suggestions to Job.

a. *God's justice and power in His dealings with man* (36:1-25). Pleading for continued patience with his words, Elihu assured Job that more was yet to be said "in God's behalf" (36:2). In self-confidence (Elihu had no problem with low self-esteem!) he stated that he would "fetch [his] knowledge from afar," meaning that he would "display the range of his knowledge,"[45] and would "ascribe righteousness to [his] Maker," that is, show that God is righteous (36:3).[46] In typical Elihu braggadocio, he affirmed that his words were not false and that he was "perfect in knowledge" (36:4).

Four times in this chapter he speaks the word "behold" to introduce a statement about God's power (36:5, 22, 26, 30). In the first of those statements, Elihu pointed out that although God is mighty, He does not lack mercy (He "does not despise"); because "He is mighty in strength of understanding" (literally, heart), He does not allow the wicked to live, something Job had denied (21:27-33); and He does exercise justice on behalf of the afflicted (36:5-6). He watches the righteous continually and even honors them like kings (36:7). However, if the righteous do suffer affliction, God uses it to point out their sins, including pride (reminiscent of 33:17 and 35:12), to teach them (cf. 33:16), and to lead them to repentance (36:8-10).

Two responses to suffering are possible for the righteous: (1) to heed what God was teaching them, and thus enjoy prosperity and pleasure (36:11), words that sound like the words of the

45. Rowley, p. 291.
46. Some scholars feel that "to my Maker" should be "from my Maker." In that case the meaning is "I will present to you righteousness [i.e., true knowledge] from my Maker" (see, e.g., Mitchell Dahood, "Chiasmus in Job: A Text-Critical and Philological Criterion," in *A Light unto My Path,* ed. H. N. Bream et al. (Philadelphia: Temple University, 1974), p. 126.

three counselors, who urged Job to repent as the means to receive blessing; (2) to refuse to listen to God's teaching, and thus to experience death (36:12). "Perish by the sword" is the expression Elihu had used earlier to refer to death (33:18, marg.). For them to "die without knowledge" meant that they died without having learned what they might have gained from their problems.

In summary, the differing attitudes of the godless and the righteous afflicted toward suffering were again cited by Elihu: (1) The godless become angry (presumably at God) for their problems; yet they refuse to turn to Him for help (cf. 35:9, 12),[47] and therefore they meet untimely deaths (36:13-14) and live a shameful existence. The phrase "among the [male] cult prostitutes" suggests a life of terrible shame, often ending in a premature death. (2) The righteous afflicted, on the other hand, are delivered (36:15a) and learn from the experience (36:15b).

Elihu then applied these points about suffering and God's justice and power to Job (36:16-25). Although difficult in the Hebrew, the verses may contain several warnings to Job: do not scoff (36:16-18), do not depend on your money or strength (36:19), do not long for death (36:20), do not turn to evil (36:21), do not suggest that God has done wrong (36:22-23), and do praise Him (36:24-25).

According to Elihu, God intended to entice Job from distress into a broad place (i.e., from the confinements of his sufferings to relief) and to give him a rich blessing, but he became loaded under God's judgment reserved for the wicked, and he became subject to condemnation and justice (36:16-17). The warning to Job, then, is to avoid anger and scoffing (the godless become angry [36:13]) and not to let "the greatness of the ransom" (the large price he is paying by his suffering) turn him aside from upright living (36:18). To attempt to alleviate his problem by buying it off,[48] by using his human efforts (a useless suggestion

47. By comparing "they are bound" (36:8) and "He binds them" (36:13), it becomes clear that God brings about the suffering, which is understandable for He seeks to use it to give correction and instruction and to induce repentance.
48. Numerous interpretations and translations are possible for 36:19a, as revealed by checking exegetical commentaries and translations. Space does not permit a detailed discussion; furthermore, the sense is not greatly altered by the various renderings.

in view of Job's poverty and illness), or by wanting to die (as Job had expressed several times) was not the answer, Elihu naively suggested (36:19-20). Instead, Job should be careful that he not turn to sin (by complaining), which seems to have been his preference to bearing his trials without complaint.

Turning Job's attention to God, Elihu urged him to note that God is exalted (literally, acts majestically) in His power,[49] is an unsurpassable Teacher, is an independent Sovereign answerable to no one, and always does right and therefore cannot rightfully be challenged by man (36:22-23). Job should therefore exalt God's work (i.e., magnify Him for what He does) rather than criticize him, for godly men have always sung praises to Him, and all mankind see and are overawed by His majestic doings, which are seen from afar (36:24-25). Job himself had spoken of the majesty of God, but still had complained because of the seeming injustice meted out to him. Elihu's point was that those two things—man's awareness of God's majesty and his murmuring against Him—should not go together. Elihu was correct; when man adores God—the majestic, powerful One, the Teacher, the Sovereign, the One whose works are majestic—he has less occasion for complaining and self-pity. Worship of God enables him to learn from his problems.

b. *God's sovereignty and benevolence in His dealings with nature* (36:26—37:24). Having mentioned God's work that man sees, Elihu then elaborated on those doings of God in nature, first in the autumn storm (36:27-33), then in the winter (37:1-13), and finally in the summer (37:17-18). The section begins with a statement about God's greatness (36:26), ends with a similar statement (37:22b-23), and includes one in the middle (37:5).

The extent of God's glorious greatness cannot be comprehended, nor can His eternity be understood (36:26; cf. 33:12b). Evaporation and rain (36:27-28), clouds and thunder (36:29), lightning and flooding of the oceans[50] (36:30)—all part of God's works—demonstrate His greatness, for man cannot begin to un-

---

49. "Power" here is the same word for Job's strength in 36:19.
50. Scholars differ on the exact meanings of "the mist" (36:27) and "the depths of the sea" (36:30).

derstand them. Those elements of the sky are used by God to bring judgment on man and to give food to men and animals, purposes that are universally acknowledgeable today (36:31). Referring again to the lightning, Elihu said that God covers His hands with it (spoken picturesquely—as if He sends bolts of lightning from His hands as easily as He would shoot darts), and the lightning hits its mark (36:32). Also thunder (the "noise" of the lightning) announces that He is present, and even the cattle are aware of an approaching storm (36:33).[51]

In view of the power and vivid nature of thunder, Elihu's heart palpitated with fear and jumped "from its place" (37:1) as he continued his majestic description of a thunderstorm (37:2-5). Thunder is often spoken of as God's voice, as it is here (37:2, 4, 5). It is so massive in its raging ("thunder" [37:2] is literally "raging") and rumbling noise that it is as if God loosened it under all the heavens; it is accompanied by His lightning "to the ends of the earth." God's thunder, like a roaring voice, follows and accompanies lightning; both are God's doings—"great things which we cannot comprehend" (37:3-5; cf. 5:9; 9:10). Job, too, had spoken of God's "mighty thunder" (26:14).

A snowfall or a heavy rain, falling at God's command, can stop man from working in his fields ("He seals the hand of every man")—and even today it can snarl traffic and keep people confined to their homes! A beautiful snowfall or a torrential downpour can lead men to contemplate the fact that those marvels are the works of the majestic God (37:6-7) .

Animals go into hibernation (37:8) when windstorms come from their chamber (the meaning of "south," spoken as if storms are stored in chambers until they are released), when the cold comes from the blowing wind ("blowing wind" is a possible meaning for the word "north"), when frost is formed by "the breath of God" (not by the violent wind, but as if by mere breathing God causes frost to settle on the earth), and when waters are frozen (37:9-10). Clouds are filled and emptied by God, and clouds and lightning change direction at His command (37:11-

---

51. The meaning of this verse too is notoriously difficult to determine in the Hebrew. For various explanations, see Barnes, 2:176-77; Pope, pp. 276-77; Reichert, p. 190; and Rowley, p. 301.

12). All those phenomena of nature in autumn and winter are purposeful and causal, not haphazard. God may use them for various purposes (37:13): to bring judgment on some (e.g., by ruining crops, flooding land or possessions, bringing death) or to benefit the earth, or as means of showing His loyalty-love to man (e.g., sunsets, snow). The second reason has no relationship to man; God often does in nature things that man knows nothing about (sending rain on the desert is only one example). "Sometimes He might have a storm, just 'for Himself.' "[52] As Job was to learn later from the Lord Himself, "God is free to do what He pleases without having to explain everything as part of His purpose for mankind."[53]

As in the first part of this fourth discourse, so here Elihu applied to Job the truths he discussed. In the next section (37:14-24), Elihu told Job that (1) he should be awed by God (37:14-18), (2) he cannot approach God (37:19-20), (3) he cannot find God (37:21-23), and (4) he must fear God (37:24).

Advising Job to "stand and consider [i.e., be still in reverence and contemplate] the wonders of God" (37:14), Elihu used a series of questions to remind Job of his inadequacies in knowledge and power. Job did not know how God controlled the lightning and made it flash (37:15), nor did he know how God could balance[54] or suspend the clouds in the air when they were so full of water. Those "wonders of one perfect in knowledge" (37:16)[55] are beyond man's comprehension. In fact, he could not even explain why his "garments are hot" in the sultry air that the hot wind from the south produced in the summer desert (37:17). Nor was he able, like God, to "spread out the skies, strong as a molten mirror" (37:18). Mirrors were made of bronze that had been heated, flattened, and polished. The cloudless summer sky appeared to be such a mirror (cf. Deut 28:23). Elihu reasoned that in view of such a sovereign God, no man could "arrange" his case before God; but that was what Job had longed to do (cf. 13:18, which translates the word "arrange" as "prepared"). Man is in-

---

52. Andersen, p. 266.
53. Ibid.
54. "Layers" is literally "balancings."
55. Elihu had used the same phrase, "perfect in knowledge" of himself (36:4).

capable of approaching God directly in his own defense "because of darkness," that is, because he is in the dark regarding God's ways. In irony Elihu challenged Job to tell them what they should say to God if any of them dared approach Him, implying that Job was unable to do so. Because Job could not comprehend the common observable actions of nature, such as the flashing of lightning, the balancing of the clouds, the coming of the hot south wind, or the blue, mirrorlike summer skies, how could he have the audacity to defend himself before God? Even if someone were merely to tell God that man wanted to speak to Him, he would in essence be saying that he wanted to be "swallowed up" (37:20). To attempt to argue a case with God in self-defense would only result in self-destruction.

Returning to the wonders of God in the sky, Elihu stated that men cannot look on the bright light (i.e., the sun; cf. 31:26) in the sky, which is cleared of clouds by the wind (37:21).[56] Barnes takes the dazzling sun to be a symbol of God, who began to appear in a coming storm.[57] Elihu may have seen the splendorous evidence of God's presence in the sky, as He approached in a whirlwind (38:1) to reveal Himself to Job. "Out of the north comes golden splendor" (37:22a) reads literally "Out of the north comes gold." Because the context (37:21) refers to the sky, it seems reasonable to assume with many Bible scholars that the gold is not the metal, but rather "golden splendor." To what, then, does the "golden splendor" refer? Some scholars suggest the color of the sun, but the sun does not come from "the north." Others suggest the Aurora Borealis, but would Elihu have seen that? Ugaritic mythology refers to the north as the residence of the gods (cf. Mount Zaphon [Isa 14:13]). Baal left his golden palace in the northern mountains of the sky, but here God comes from the north in splendor far exceeding that of the pagan god.[58] For He—the Almighty One—comes in "awesome majesty." By saying that He is the Almighty whom "we cannot find" (37: 23), Elihu was again chiding Job for his attempts to discover God

---

56. Some scholars suggest that the first part of 37:21 means that man cannot see the sun because it is obscured by the clouds, but the above seems preferable.
57. Barnes, 2:188-89.
58. See Pope, pp. 286-87.

161

(9:11; 23:3-4, 8-9) so that he might present his case and be delivered. In the rising crescendo of his final words, spoken in awe of God's majestic splendor, Elihu affirmed God's two characteristics that he had been expounding in his speeches—His sovereignty ("He is exalted in power") and His justice ("He will not do violence to justice and abundant righteousness") (37:23). His remarks about God's justice opposed Job's repeated accusation that God is unjust (7:20; 9:17, 20-24; 10:2-3; 13:24; 16:9, 12, 17; 19:6-12; 27:2; 30:19-23), though Job was certainly aware of God's sovereignty and power (e.g., 9:4-12; 10:16; 12:13-25; 23:13-16; 26:5-14; 28:23-28).

Elihu's final recommendation to Job was that he fear God, for such an awesome Sovereign, full of power and justice, would not look on any human being who considers himself wise. Job had said that *God* is "wise in heart" (9:4), so how could he think of himself as wise? The true essence of wisdom is reverential awe before God, as Job himself had affirmed (28:28). Elihu in his final sentence thus again associated himself with the three friends by considering Job to be conceited. Before such a mighty God, Job should bow in worship and humility.

Elihu thus prepared the way for God to speak. Although he stressed aspects of suffering and of the character of God beyond those mentioned by Eliphaz, Bildad, and Zophar, he did not have total insight into Job's situation. In fact, he could not have such complete insight. No man could. It was therefore necessary that God speak.

12

God's Science Quiz

F. GOD'S CONFRONTATION (38:1—42:6)

After Elihu finished speaking, God broke in and addressed Job "out of the whirlwind" (38:1). The sufferer's repetitious plea that God answer him was granted. "Let me speak, then reply to me" (13:22) and "Let the Almighty answer me!" (31:35) are two of Job's persistent demands for communication from God. Having bemoaned the absence of an arbiter (9:33), having longed for a witness or advocate (16:19), and having expressed assurance of a Redeemer who would vindicate his cause after death (19:25), Job was confronted by God Himself.

And what a confrontation it was! In content as well as timing it was unlike what Job expected. Nothing was said about Job's suffering; no discussion was included about the theology of evil; nor was even any extensive answer given to the brash charges the patriarch had made about the Sovereign's injustices (only two brief questions were asked [40:2, 8]). Instead of answering questions, God asked them! That alone was evidence of His sovereignty, of the correctness of Elihu's advice that men should fear Him (37:24).

Divine justice was the all-consuming concern in the four-against-one debates. Job denied it; the four defended it; but God did neither. He ignored it (except for 40:2, 8) and went instead to the subject of His creative power and wise, benevolent control.

God was not on the witness stand; Job was! From the agony of his seated posture among the ashes—scraping his skin with a potsherd and suffering from the weight of grief over the loss of family, possessions, health, and friends—Job was confronted by the divine Interrogator with more than seventy unanswerable

163

questions whose subject matter ranged from the constellations to the clods, from the beasts to the birds. God showed Job that the wonders of His handiwork in outer space, in the sky, and on the earth were beyond Job's grasp. And the animals and birds, cared for by God, were not under Job's command or even intended for his use.[1]

The purpose was clear: Job was put in his place before God; he was shown to be ignorant and impotent in contrast to the Sovereign's wisdom and power. If he could not comprehend or control God's government in nature, how could he hope to comprehend or control the Lord's ways with man?

The confrontation includes God's first speech (38:1—40:2), followed by Job's response of humility (40:3-5), and God's second speech (40:6—41:34), followed by Job's response of repentance (42:1-6). The section "reaches dazzling heights of poetic splendour."[2] In fact, the first speech "transcends all other descriptions of the wonders of creation or the greatness of the Creator, which are to be found either in the Bible or elsewhere."[3]

1. God's first speech (38:1—40:2)

a. God challenged Job (38:1-3). In the Bible, God's appearances were often accompanied by storms, thus dramatizing the awesomeness of the occasion (e.g., Exod 19:16-17; 1 Kings 19:11-13; Isa 6:4; Ezek 1:4; Zech 9:14). "Like his human predecessors [God] begins his response with a retort challenging his opponent's insights."[4] God's opening question, "Who is this that darkens counsel by words without knowledge?" (38:2), derided Job for his perversion and ignorance of God's design for the universe ("counsel" means "plan or design"). This question may ironically allude to the darkness of the windstorm.[5] As a friend of God, Job would have been expected to defend and vindicate God's ways to others. But instead, his charge that God's dealings

1. Robert Gordis, *Poets, Prophets, and Sages* (Bloomington, Ind.: Indiana U., 1971), p. 293.
2. Victor E. Reichert, *Job*, p. 195.
3. S. R. Driver, *Introduction to the Literature of the Old Testament*, rev. ed. (New York: Scribner's, 1914), p. 427.
4. Norman C. Habel, *The Book of Job* (New York: Cambridge U., 1975), pp. 201-2.
5. Samuel Terrien, "The Yahweh Speeches and Job's Responses," *Review and Expositor* 68 (1971):501.

were unjust, that God was his enemy, made His designs appear dark and severe. His words were "without knowledge," that is, without a true awareness of the facts, without an understanding of God's and Satan's heavenly controversy, which had precipitated Job's trial. Likewise, believers today should not presume to know fully God's ways, His "counsel" (or plan) for them. To act on inadequate knowledge of divine purposes is to run the risk of beclouding and misrepresenting His intents.

The reproof of Job's presumption was followed by God's challenge to him to "gird up [his] loins like a man" (38:3). When undertaking a strenuous task such as running, working, or fighting, a man in biblical times would gather up his flowing robe and tuck it into a sash-belt (Exod 12:11; 1 Kings 18:46).[6] Thus this figure of speech suggests that Job was to be alert and prepared for a difficult task—that of explaining God's ways in nature. Because Job had questioned God's doings and accused Him of wrongdoing, he was here challenged to support those claims. Job the plaintiff had suddenly become the defendant!

b. *God questioned Job regarding two areas of creation* (38:4—39:30). God had said, "I will ask you, and you instruct Me" (38:3b). Those questions then began immediately—a series of dozens of inquiries filled with irony and stated not with cruelty but with firmness. They demonstrated that Job's presumptuous criticisms had darkened rather than shed light on God's plans.

God's science quiz included questions on cosmology, oceanography, meteorology, astronomy, and zoology. Items in the physical world related to the earth (38:4-7); the oceans (38:8-11); the dawn (38:12-15); the depths of the ocean and Sheol (38:16-17); the width of the earth (38:18); light and darkness (38:19-21); atmospheric elements, including snow and hail, light and wind, rain, dew, ice, and frost (38:22-30); stars (38:31-33); and clouds and lightning (38:34-38). The second list included references to ten beasts and birds, all of which are undomesticated except the horse: lion (38:39-40), raven (38:41), mountain goat (39:1-4), deer (also 39:1-4), wild donkey (39:5-8), wild

6. It is unlikely that belt-wrestling in a court is intended here, as Cyrus Gordon suggests ("Belt-Wrestling in the Bible World," *Hebrew Union College Annual* 23 [1950-51]:131-36), for nowhere else in Scripture is it used in that way.

165

ox (39:9-12), ostrich (39:13-18), horse (39:19-25), hawk (39:26), and eagle (39:27-30).

The creation of the earth (38:4-7) was depicted as the construction of a building, with its foundation, dimensions (the meaning of "measurements"), measuring line, footings (the meaning of "bases"; the earth was figuratively presented as having pillars sunk into sockets), and cornerstone. By asking Job "Where were you [when all this was accomplished]?" and by challenging Job to tell who did it all, God immediately demonstrated Job's ignorance and insignificance. Of course Job knew that God had created the earth, but that knowledge was not from personal observation. Man, created after the earth had been made, was not present and therefore Job could not have advised God or have understood what took place. Unable to have done those things, how could Job possibly hope to advise God now? His deficiency of the knowledge of the earth's origin disqualified Job from governing the earth.

God's building task was accompanied by singing and joy (38:7). The "morning stars" may be another term for the "sons of God," who are clearly angels (cf. 1:6), or they may be stars (like Venus and Mercury [cf. 3:9]) spoken of poetically as if they sang. Stars and angels are mentioned together (Psalm 148:2-3); both are commanded to praise the Lord. They were present at the founding of the earth, and would know the answers to God's questions; but man, though the apex of God's creation, is less informed on this matter than the stars and angels.

The origin of the oceans (38:8-11) was described by God in the poetic language of childbirth. In Mesopotamian and Ugaritic mythology, the sea is pictured as an adversary to be defeated by the gods, a great chaotic monster, which the author of Job had alluded to already (3:8; 7:12; 9:13; 26:12). But here "the sea is not God's adversary; it is a giant baby, just born, that had to be confined at the moment of birth."[7] Verse 8 actually mixes the metaphor, however, because the raging of the water, pictured as bursting forth from the womb, needed to be restrained by doors. The earth's shorelines are thus presented as gates that

7. Matitiahu Tsevat, "The Meaning of the Book of Job," *Hebrew Union College Annual* 77 (1966):84.

hold back water at a dam (cf. Gen 1:9). The broken clouds were the baby's garment, and darkness was its swaddling clothes (38:9). Its limits were like a double door and a bolt (i.e., a safety bar across a city gate) holding it back in obedience to God's order: "Thus far you shall come, but no farther; and here shall your proud waves stop" (38:11). "Proud waves" is literally "the pride of your waves"; it portrays the waves as advancing in arrogant self-confidence but being stopped by God's power. "The sea, born clothed and confined to its cosmic playpen, is now given the paternal command never to cross the appointed boundaries."[8] Job had nothing to do with this majestic work, which was performed only by God.

The coming of the dawn (38:12-15), which God brings about every day, is something Job had never done in his entire lifetime. God's justice is evident even in the sunrise, for the dawn, which knows "its place" (knowing where to rise each morning) takes hold of the ends of the earth as if the darkness were a blanket over the globe and shakes the wicked out of it (38:13). Dawn exposes and disperses the evildoers, who prefer darkness to light (John 3:19). As the sun comes up, it reveals the contours of the earth, causing it to appear changed, as clay is suddenly changed when impressed by a seal (38:14a). The meaning of the clause, "they stand forth like a garment" (38:14b) is unclear, but it may indicate that the earth's features stand out as if the earth had put on a colorful garment. The blanket of darkness is taken off, and the bright garment of light is put on. The "light" that the wicked[9] prefer is darkness (as Job himself had stated [24:13-17]), and the dawn withholds it from them and prevents them from carrying out their violent purposes ("the uplifted arm is broken" [38:15]).

Not only was Job ignorant of the origin of the earth and incapable of controlling the sea or commanding the morning dawn, but also he was ignorant of things he could not see. The oceans

---

8. Habel, p. 205.
9. It is not necessary to change "the wicked" to "Dog-stars" (the Canis major and Canis minor constellations) as G. R. Driver does ("Two Astronomical Passages in the Old Testament," *Journal of Theological Studies* 4 [1953]: 208-12), nor "the uplifted arm" to "the Navigator's line," the line of stars extending like a bent arm across the sky from the horizon to the zenith.

on the earth, the dawn over the earth, the subterranean waters under the earth—all were beyond Job's reach, knowledge, and control. The fountains that seem to exist at subterranean depths and the deep places at the bottom of the ocean were unknown to Job. He had no way of getting to those fountains or walking in those recesses. They were hidden to him. But even more foreboding and inaccessible was death, pictured as having gates and being the realm of darkness (38:17). Job had not seen those gates, for he felt that if he had he could not have returned to tell about them (7:9; 10:21). The width of the earth (38:18) was also indeterminable.

Light and darkness are each depicted as having dwelling places, territories, houses (38:19-21). Light seems to come in the morning from someplace it has been staying and to return to it in the evening. Darkness, too, goes to and comes from an apparent abode. Job, however, was totally incapable of following either of them to its home to see where it goes. In 38:21, God broke in with a statement of biting irony. The suggestion that Job surely knew the answers to all these questions was God's way of strongly remonstrating Job—because he presumed to question God's governing of the universe, when in reality he could not answer even one of the questions. The reason Job could not know is that he was a latecomer, not having been born at the time God had established His cosmos and set it in motion.

In the next section (38:22-30), the Master of the universe quizzed Job about several elements pertaining to the weather—elements that are irregular and spasmodic in their appearances compared to the daily appearance of the dawn and of light and darkness—and about the perennial existence of the oceans, the ocean depths, and death. The snow and hail appear to be kept in storehouses and released by God when He so desires. He uses them in times of distress, particularly war, in order to help defeat the enemy of His people. In Joshua's defeat of the Gibeonites, God sent hailstones that killed the escaping enemy (Josh 10:11; also see Exod 9:22-26; Isa 30:30; Ezek 13:13; 38:22; Hag 2:17; Rev 16:21).

If the light (38:24) is the sun, the dispersing of its rays is here set forth in contrast to its dwelling (38:19). The word for "light," however, may indicate lightning, as it does earlier (37:11). If the word here refers to lightning, the meaning is that the lightning flashes are diversified, and Job could not know where they would go. Likewise, Job was ignorant of the scattering movements of the east wind (38:24b).

Again returning to the question "Who?"[10] the Lord asked Job (38:25) to tell who cleft a channel for the flood (i.e., a path in the sky through which the flood waters could pour down), or a path for the thunderbolt (cf. Job's earlier words [28:26]). Job could not tell who does those things because they are accomplished by God without any evidence of a person at hand. Nor could Job understand the purpose of sending rain on the desert and causing grass to sprout.

Job was also ignorant of the origin of rain, dew, ice, and frost (38:28-30). In beautiful poetic style, God again used the figure of childbirth (as in 38:9), in asking Job if the rain has a father,[11] and who gave birth to dew, ice, and frost. Only God can change water to a stonelike hardness and cause the surface of the deep waters to solidify.

Job knew that God made the Pleiades, Orion, and Bear constellations (see 9:9), but here God showed Job his impotence by asking if he were able to hold together the cluster of stars in the Pleiades in the east and west, or, in an opposite vein, to loosen the bands of Orion in the south, or to guide the Bear (the Big Dipper) in the north. The precise meaning of the Hebrew word translated "constellation" (38:32) is difficult to determine, but it is clear from the context that it refers to a group of stars.

Job's ignorance also extended to the "ordinances of the heavens," the laws or principles by which the stars and the sun and moon are governed (38:33). His inability to control nature was also evident in that he could not command the clouds to rain or tell lightning bolts where to go as if they were his messengers ready to serve him (38:35; cf. his inability to command the dawn

10. God introduced His questions to Job in numerous ways: Where were you, Who, Have you, Where is, Can you, Do you know, Will you, etc.
11. This may possibly be an allusion to and a polemic against the Canaanite myth that viewed rain as the semen of the gods, from which grew vegetable life.

[38:12]). "Innermost being" (38:36) has been rendered "Thoth" (the Egyptian god of wisdom), the bird ibis, the star Procyon, etc. The word "mind" (38:36*b*) has been translated "Sekwi" (another Egyptian god), "rooster," "mist," "meteor," etc. Although it is difficult to determine the words' meanings with certainty, two alternatives seem preferable: (1) retain the renderings "innermost being" and "mind," which translation would not be totally impossible, for the verse, placed in the middle of a five-verse paragraph, could justifiably change the subject for the purpose of emphasis, or (2) translate the words "cloud layers" (the first word in question comes from a verb meaning to cover over or spread over) and "celestial phenomenon," which would fit the context of the discussion on clouds (38:34-38). If the second alternative were chosen, God's question to Job was then intended to demonstrate that no man directs these phenomena of the sky; they operate as if they had minds of their own.

The clouds are so numerous and unending that they cannot be counted. Nor is it possible for anyone to pour out rain as if he were tilting waterskins from the heavens so that the soil would be hardened into mud, and clods would stick together (38:37-38).

God's nature quiz then turned to the animal world (38:39—39:30). Although these ten animals are seemingly chosen at random, they do include the ferocious, the helpless, the shy, the strong, the bizarre, the wild. Unusual powers and abilities are exhibited in this living museum of natural history: to pounce or prey, to soar in the sky, to live in mountains, to live in deserts, to refuse domestication, to run at high speeds, to engage in battle fearlessly, to build nests on mountain crags. All the examples exhibit the creative genius and providential care of God. His concern for these animals demonstrates that His domain exceeds that of man's immediate needs, thus further demonstrating the gap between God's designs and man's. The creation of these animals, most of which are useless to man, suggests "a superfluous element of luxury in the divine bounty."[12]

God's questions about these six beasts and four birds are grouped in twos: Questions about the first two animals pertain to providing food for them; questions about the next two relate to

12. Terrien, p. 502.

their giving birth to their young; the queries about animals five and six have to do with freedom, the next two with out-of-the-ordinary ways, and the last two with flight. It is fitting that the list begins with the lion, the king of the beasts, and concludes with the eagle, the king of the birds.

God said that Job could not successfully hunt down prey for lions or satisfy the voracious appetites of young lions waiting for him in their dens (38:39-40). In fact, for his own safety he would want to have nothing to do with them. Nor would he be capable of furnishing nourishment for the helpless, despised raven and its screeching young (38:41).

Mountain goats and deer give birth to their young without Job's having any knowledge of their gestation period (39:1-2). Hidden from civilized man, these mountain creatures bear with ease their young, who soon become strong, grow up, and leave their parents, ready to fend for themselves.

Nor did Job give the wild donkey its freedom and its desire to live in the desert (cf. 24:5) and the salt land, the habitat given to it by God (39:5-6). Free to roam in the desert, the donkey instinctively avoids the city. "The freedom of the open country is more exciting to the wild ass than all the hubbub of the city."[13] He is so far removed from man that he does not hear "the shoutings of the driver." He roams over vast territory, including mountains, to find food—any green thing will do. Thus his survival is dependent on God's provision (39:7-8).

The freedom of the wild donkey was not given by Job; nor on the other hand was he able to tame the wild ox (39:9-12). "Extinct since 1627, this enormous animal was the most powerful of all hoofed beasts, exceeded in size only by the hippopotamus and elephant.[14] Known for its strength and its strong horns, it is mentioned nine times in the Old Testament (Num 23:22; 24:8; Deut 33:17; Job 39:9, 10; Psalms 22:21; 29:6; 92:10; Isa 34:7). As the wild donkey contrasted with the domesticated donkey, so here the wild ox is distinct from the domesticated ox. "It was hunted by the Assyrians and is probably to be identified with the aurochs."[15]

13. H. H. Rowley, *Job*, p. 319.
14. Francis I. Andersen, *Job: An Introduction and Commentary*, p. 281.
15. Rowley, p. 319. "Unicorn" (KJV) wrongly suggests the one-horned, mythological oryx.

Although the unusual strength of the wild ox would have made it desirable for serving man, it resisted efforts toward domestication. It would not even spend one night in the barn with its domesticated cousin, the cow, nor could Job use it for plowing or harrowing (39:9-10). Although great in strength, it could not be trusted with man's work or relied on to take sheaves of grain to the farmer's threshing floor (39:11-12). Because Job could not effect so small a change as taming a wild ox and using it in his farming, the implication becomes explicit: Job certainly could not alter the Creator's ways or manage His universe!

The next paragraph (39:13-18) differs from the others in that it discusses a bizarre bird, the ostrich, and has all declarative statements rather than questions (39:13 [KJV] is the one exception). Verse 13 has been translated in numerous ways in an effort to render the difficult Hebrew. The word translated "love" is from the word for devotion and may be intended as a reference to the stork, a loving or devoted bird (cf. Lev 11:19; Psalm 104:17; Jer 8:7), thus contrasting the ostrich with the stork. Understood in this way, the verse may read, "The ostriches' wings flap joyously but are they the pinions and plumage of the stork?"[16]

The odd-featured ostrich is the largest living bird, weighing up to three hundred pounds and reaching a height of seven or eight feet. It is the only bird with two toes (all other birds have three or four), and the only bird with eyelashes. Although it has wings, it cannot fly, and it builds its nest in the sand rather than in a tree or rocky crag. Its long neck, covered with down instead of feathers, and its huge eyes resemble a periscope watching for danger. It is commonly supposed that the mother ostrich is indifferent to her eggs, and this is sustained by the NASB: "she abandons her eggs to the earth" (39:14). However, the ostrich puts[17] them in a shallow hole in the sand, usually dug out by the male, covers them with sand, and sits on them in order to protect them from predators. Although "she forgets that a foot may crush them" (39:15a) may seem to suggest that she ignores her eggs, the point

16. For a discussion of the translation problems, see Rowley, p. 321.
17. The translation "puts" is preferred to "abandons" because of a Ugaritic parallel, as reported by Mitchell J. Dahood, "The Root עזב II in Job," *Journal of Biblical Literature* 78 (1959):307-8.

is that she leaves some eggs out of the nest to serve as food for the newly hatched brood.

"She treats her young cruelly, as if they were not hers" (39: 16a) appears to contradict the statement that "the parents display great solicitude for their agile little chicks."[18] However, when chased by hunters, "the adult birds often run away, hoping to draw off the intruders, while the chicks lie flat on the ground."[19] In other words, this peculiar action signals to man a neglect of its young, when in actuality it is the opposite. Moreover, because several ostrich hens often lay their eggs together in one sand nest, it becomes difficult for any one hen to distinguish her own. Therefore, it seems to man that the ostrich's giving birth to its young is all in vain, for she seems strangely unconcerned (39: 16b).

The stupidity of the ostrich (39:17) is proverbial among the Arabs.[20] This lack of wisdom and understanding, attributed to God, is illustrated by Pliny, who, in his *Natural History,* referred to ostriches' hiding their heads and necks in a bush, thinking they were safe because they could see nothing.[21] It may also be reflected in the practice of the ostrich to run in a large circular path, thus enabling a hunter eventually to track it down.

Yet in spite of its stupidity, the ostrich can run at the remarkably high speed of forty miles per hour, outstripping even swift horses (39:18). The phrase "when she lifts herself on high" (39:18a) refers to an ostrich's lifting its head, extending its rudimentary wings for balance, and taking giant strides of twelve to fifteen feet while running.

God's intentional creation of such a peculiar bird, inferior to other animals in wisdom and yet greater than others in speed, illustrates again His sovereign ways. If God chooses to make a ridiculous kind of bird, He can do so, and Job could do nothing about it!

Mention of the horse in contrast to the ostrich (39:18) leads naturally to a vivid description of the war horse (39:19-25). The

18. *Encyclopaedia Britannica,* 1969 ed., 16:1150.
19. George Cansdale, *Animals of Bible Lands* (London: Paternoster, 1970), p. 193.
20. See Marvin H. Pope, *Job,* p. 310.
21. Cansdale, p. 193.

spirited nature of the poetic paragraph matches the vitality of the horse itself. As in the preceding paragraph, declarative descriptions outnumber the questions. Job, though superior as a man to the animal kingdom, was unable to provide the horse with its strength or its mane (39:19) and could not make it "leap like the locust" (39:20a).[22] In its spirited eagerness, the horse snorts terribly and paws vigorously, seeming to rejoice "in his strength" (39:20-21). Fearless in its charge into battle, it is undaunted by weapons such as the sword (39:21-22). The movements of the rider's quiver of arrows and his spear and javelin against the horse's side seem to abet the animal on (39:23). He excitedly prances into the ground as if he would swallow it up,[23] and hearing the trumpet, which signals the battle charge, he can hardly stand still. He says "Aha!" (meaning that he impatiently neighs), he smells the battle at a distance, and he hears the thunder (i.e., war shouts) of the captains, and the shouting (39:24-25).

The fact that even the one domesticated animal in this catena of natural history is strong and fierce further underscores Job's incompetence. Because Job is inferior to the horse, with its dauntless lust for battle, he is unquestionably inferior to the horse's Creator. The horse's "majesty, energy, strength, impatience for the battle, and spirit, were proofs of the greatness of Him who had made him. . . ."[24]

The hawk, in its annual migration to the south, soars instinctively and without any help from Job (39:26). On the other hand, the eagle builds its nest at high altitudes on inaccessible mountain cliffs and with keen sight spies food at great distances away (39:27-29). The carcass-devouring, bloodsucking practice of its young suggests that this bird is the griffon-vulture rather than the eagle.[25]

c. *God challenged Job to reply* (40:1-2). God's first speech, having begun with a challenge, also ended with one: "Will the faultfinder contend with the Almighty? Let him who reproves

22. "Leap" means "quiver or shake," thus possibly referring to the horse's galloping or agile movement, similar to locusts (cf. Joel 2:4-5).
23. "He swallows up the ground" is the literal rendering for "he races over the ground."
24. Albert Barnes, *Notes, Critical, Illustrative, and Practical, on the Book of Job,* 2:235.
25. Cf. Cansdale, p. 144.

174

God answer it" (40:2). The noun "faultfinder" occurs only here in the Old Testament, but it comes from a common verb meaning "to admonish or correct." At least twice (10:2; 23:6a) Job had accused God of contending with him (bringing a court case against him), but now God turned the accusation around. This aligns with Elihu's question, "Why do you complain [present an indictment] against Him?" (33:13). Now that Job had seen God's parade of power evidenced in nature, how could he indict God? Job was deficient in knowledge regarding God's ways and incompetent to control nature, so how could he presume to expect God to report to him?

The word "reproves" (40:2b) means "to argue." It too had been used by Job; he had expressed both his desire and his determination to argue with God (13:3, 15). In brevity, unlike Job's prolixity, God simply informed Job that an arguer with the Sovereign would need to answer the question raised in the preceding sentence.[26]

2. *Job's first reply to God* (40:3-5)

Confronted with God's yes-or-no question, "Will you continue to indict Me for injustice?" the faultfinder admitted to his insignificance[27] and to his inability to respond to God (40:4). His former self-confidence ("Then call, and I will answer" [13:22a]) now shriveled to humility ("What can I reply to Thee?"). Job's words amounted to an admission by Job that he was unable to instruct God as God had challenged him to do (38:3). Job had come almost full circle—from hesitation to confront God ("How then can I answer Him?" [9:14]) through confidence ("I will answer" [13:22a]) and a final sweep of assertiveness ("Like a prince I would approach Him" [31:37]) to humbled inability to respond.

Silence in the Almighty's presence was exhibited by Job's gesture of placing his hand on his mouth—a response that he had advised for his counselors (21:5). He had repeated himself be-

---

26. Some scholars, however, view the "it" (40:2b) as referring to "the glory of Creation, the display of Divine omnipotence" set forth in chapters 38 and 39 (e.g., Reichert, p. 209).

27. "Vile" (KJV) conveys the wrong impression, for the Hebrew for "insignificant" means "to be trifling or small."

fore God—" Once I have spoken, . . . even twice" (40:5; cf. 33:14), but now any further elaboration was unnecessary. Job said, "I will add no more." He was only admitting that he need not repeat himself, not that he had said too much. Because Job did not admit to any sin, God found it necessary to continue with a second speech, to speak not only once, but twice.

3. God's second speech (40:6—41:34)

God's second speech followed a pattern similar to that of the first: a challenge to Job and a questioning of Job regarding nature, followed by a reply from Job. Whereas the first speech reviewed two areas of creation, the inanimate and animate, the second oration presented two animals of creation, Behemoth and Leviathan.

a. *God challenged Job* (40:6-14). God's approach here began as His first confrontation had begun: out of the whirlwind (the word "storm" [40:6] is the same as "whirlwind" [38:1]) and with the demand that Job face up to the strenuous presentation and then instruct God if he were able to do so (40:6-7).

The subject of justice, which Job had come back to repeatedly, was touched on by God only briefly. God asked, "Will you really annul [literally, break or render ineffectual] My judgment? Will you condemn Me that you may be justified?" (40:8). Job had let his defense of his integrity lead him astray, to the extreme of blaming God. But any mortal's alleged superiority to God's justice must be accompanied by a similar superiority of power. And yet God's next question (40:9) demonstrated not only Job's lack of superiority, but also his lack of equality. Job did not have an arm like God's ("arm" being the biblical symbol of strength [Psalm 89:13]) or even a voice (thunder) like His.

Pursuing this thought, God in piercing irony challenged Job to imagine himself in control of the universe, to " 'play God' and see if he could do better."[28] His first responsibility was to dress the part, putting on God's "eminence and dignity . . . honor and majesty" (40:10; cf. Psalms 93:1; 104:1). His assignment would then be to bring down the proud and the wicked in an un-

28. L. D. Johnson, *Out of the Whirlwind: The Major Message of Job*, p. 64.

176

leashed[29] display of his anger, humiliating them just by looking at them, demolishing them, and burying them in the ground, out of sight[30] (40:11-13). If Job could perform this administrative function, which he had accused God of neglecting,[31] God would praise Job as one superior to Him and Job could save himself (40:14). Then neither God nor even a mediator (9:33) would be necessary.[32]

Because Job was unable to assume God's managerial responsibilities over the wicked, it became clear that he could not save himself. Hence it follows that man, dependent on God, must not question Him, even though he cannot fully comprehend His ways.

b. *God questioned Job regarding two animals of creation* (40: 15—41:34). In His first speech, God presented Job with a panorama of nature, thus illustrating the Lord's creative variety in the universe. Here, however, the focus is on only two animals, generally considered the strangest on land and the wildest in the sea. The purpose in this zoom-lens photography of Behemoth (40:15-24) and Leviathan (chap. 41) was the same as in the first speech: to impress Job with his feeble puniness in contrast to the strength evident in natural creation and thus to impress Job with God's majestic power. This purpose is evident in the questions God inserted in His discussion on Leviathan: "Who then is he that can stand before Me? Who has given to Me that I should repay him?" (41:10*b*, 11*a*).

Scholars vary in their identification of these creatures, and they also vary in their opinions as to whether the creatures were real or mythological. Those scholars who view them as creatures of Canaanite myths point to parallels in ancient mythological literature, to the fanciful language that describes Leviathan (e.g., 41:18-22), and to the references to Leviathan in Job (3:8) and elsewhere in the Bible as a mythological monster. For other scholars, it seems preferable to view these animals as actual creatures because (a) God said that He made Behemoth (40:15)

29. "Pour out" (40:11) is the word "scatter," used by Elihu of God's scattering of ("He disperses") the lightning (37:11*b*).
30. "The hidden place" refers to the grave.
31. Habel, p. 220.
32. "Hand" (40:14) and "arm" (40:9) pull this passage together.

and Leviathan (Psalm 104:26b), (b) the detailed description of the anatomy of each animal suggests real animals, (c) the animals of myths were based on actual animals, although features may have been combined or exaggerated, as in the seven-headed deity, Leviathan, (d) the ten animals listed in God's first speech are actual, and (e) both animals in the second speech are mentioned elsewhere in Scripture apart from mythological connotations (e.g., Psalm 104:26; Joel 1:20, where the word translated "beasts" is the word "Behemoth"). If they are real, then the smoke from Leviathan's nostrils and fire from his mouth may be explained as poetic hyperbole.

God invited Job to consider Behemoth a being on a level with Job as a fellow creature: "Which I made as well as you" (40:15). He then described his diet (40:15b), physical strength (40:16-18), habitat (40:20-23), and fierceness (40:24). The word "Behemoth" is the plural of *beast*. Because the descriptions pertain to a single animal, it is safely assumed that the plural form of his name points to the animal's superlative strength. But what is Behemoth? Suggestions include (a) the elephant[33] (because his tail is likened to a cedar [40:17]; because he is one of the strongest animals known; because his nose cannot be trapped [40:24, marg.]); (b) the extinct hornless rhinoceros,[34] (c) the plant-eating brontosaurus dinosaur (because of its massive bodily strength, the bending of its tail like a cedar, and its habitat), some of which may have survived the Flood,[35] (d) the water buffalo[36] (because of its habitat among the marshes), and (e) the hippopotamus (because of its weight, strength, habitat among watery plants, and the difficulty of catching it "by the eyes"[37] or nose when only those parts of its head show above water [40:24]). The hippopotamus, the animal traditionally identified with Behemoth, seems as likely as the others or more so, because it was known in the ancient Near East and because Egyptian rec-

33. R. Laird Harris, "The Book of Job and Its Doctrine of God," *Grace Journal* 13 (Fall 1976): 20-21.
34. Bernard Northrup, "Light on the Ice Age," *Bible-Science Newsletter,* June 1976, p. 4.
35. "Dinosaurs and the Bible," *Five Minutes with the Bible & Science* (supplement to *Bible-Science Newsletter*), May 1976, n.p.
36. B. Coureyer, "Qui est Behemoth?" *Revue Biblique* 82 (1975):418-43.
37. This wording is preferable over "when he is on watch."

ords picture hippos being hunted with harpoons and barbed hooks.

The grass diet of Behemoth (40:15) conforms to the fact that the hippopotamus is strictly herbivorous. The beast's strength is evident in its loins, stomach muscles, tail, and thighs, and in its metallike bones (40:16-18). The bending of its tail like a cedar (40:17a) is strange because the hippopotamus's tail is so small. However, Ugaritic parallels indicate that the sentence may read, "His tail is stiff [or stiffens] like a cedar."[38]

As "the first of the ways of God" (40:19), Behemoth is first in rank in God's animal creation, not first chronologically, but one of the first in size and strength. (The adult hippopotamus weighs up to eight thousand pounds.) "Let his maker bring near his sword" (40:19b) is an inadequate rendering of a difficult line in Hebrew. Reichert reports that Jewish rabbis interpreted the line to mean that only God (Behemoth's Maker) dare go near it with a sword (for the purpose of hand combat).[39] The next clause ("the mountains bring him food" [40:20a]) "presents some difficulty, although hippopotami do venture to forage."[40] Because the beast eats only vegetation, other animals can play near him without fear (40:20b). He rests in the shade of the lotus plant ("a low thorny shrub,"[41] not the water lily), the reeds of the marsh, and willows. The turbulent river does not disturb him (suggesting his marshy habitat), even if it comes up to his mouth. This latter point seems more like a reference to the hippopotamus than to the elephant, rhinoceros, or brontosaurus (could a normal surging river reach a depth up to the nose of the brontosaurus?). The Hebrew word for "the Jordan" (40:23b) is literally "a Jordan" and is therefore simply "an illustration of a swift running current."[42]

Job's weakness in contrast to this beast's strength is emphasized by God's concluding question to the chapter (40:24). No one can capture him "by the eyes" (a possible meaning, as sug-

---

38. Harris makes the surprising suggestion that "tail" means the elephant's trunk (p. 20), but how does the trunk stiffen?
39. Reichert, p. 212.
40. Andersen, p. 289. Also see Pope, p. 325.
41. Reichert, p. 213.
42. Rowley, p. 331.

gested earlier, of "when he is on watch") or by the nose when only those small parts of his massive body are above water.

Leviathan has been variously interpreted as the seven-headed sea monster Lotan of Ugaritic mythology,[43] the whale, the dolphin, a marine dinosaur that survived the Flood,[44] and the crocodile. The detailed description of Leviathan's anatomy and man's attempts to capture him point to an actual creature known by Job. The whale and dolphin do not seem to fit those descriptions, and identifying the animals of God's second speech with land and marine dinosaurs depends on a chronology that places Job within only a few hundred years of the Flood. Although that chronology is possible, it may be tenuous.

If Leviathan is the crocodile, as viewed by many commentators, then the two final creatures exhibited by God have some striking parallels (assuming Behemoth is the hippopotamus). Both are amphibious, both live in marshes and rivers, both are huge in size (both attaining a length of about twelve feet), both have skins difficult for man's weapons to penetrate, both are difficult to capture, both enjoy floating in the water with only their eyes and nostrils above the surface, and both are speedy and vicious (the normally mild hippo can lumber ahead with great speed when wounded or when its young are molested). Both animals, more than the ten animals of the desert and mountains (38:39—39: 30), were dreaded by man. The ten zoological creatures live on the land and in the sky, whereas here the two live on land and sea, though primarily the latter. The fact that the discussion of Leviathan is longer than that of any of the other animals and the fact that the crocodile is the most vicious of all the animals recounted by God, somtimes preying even on man, gives chapter 41 a climactic character.

God's account of Leviathan includes these parts: the crocodile's inability to be captured by fishing equipment and to be used by man (41:1-11), the crocodile's awesome anatomy (41:12-25), and the crocodile's inability to be captured by hunting equipment

43. Pope, pp. 329-31; and others.
44. "Dinosaurs and the Bible," n.p., suggests the Allosaurus or Tyrannosaurus rex; and George Mulfinger, Jr., suggests the Plesioaurus or Mosasaurus ("Dinosaurs—The Facts Support Creation," *Faith*, May-June 1976, p. 18).

(41:26-34). Each section concludes with statements about man's fear of the animal (41:9-11, 25, 33-34).

The use of only questions in 41:1-7 (along with a few others [41:9-11, 13-14]) reflects the style used in most of God's speech to Job.

Mere fishhooks, cords, ropes, and hooks are inadequate for fishing for crocodiles (41:1-2). Some readers have questioned the reference to the crocodile's tongue (41:1*b*), but the crocodile does have a tongue, although it is attached to the lower jaw. The fierce crocodile is not so easily tamed that it will plead like a prisoner to be released (41:3). Nor will it agree to being domesticated for the purpose of serving man (41:4); nor can man play with it like a pet bird (41:5). Furthermore, merchants will be unable to bargain over it and divide it, for it will not very often be captured (41:6). Returning to man's fishing efforts, God added that even larger equipment such as harpoons and fishing spears will be ineffectual (41:7). So fierce is this reptile that God in humorous irony reminded Job that attempting to capture a crocodile by hand is unthinkable: "Lay your hand on him; remember the battle; you will not do it again!" (41:8). Any hope of capturing him is useless, for man is overwhelmed even at the sight of the crocodile (41:9). No wonder, then, that no one wants to awaken him if he does see the animal (41:10*a*). Job could not challenge the crocodile successfully, so he certainly could not challenge God, the amphibian's Maker (41:10*b*). Furthermore, man can give nothing to God (for everything under heaven belongs to Him) and therefore cannot obligate God to pay him back (41:11). The crocodile thus became a divine object lesson, teaching Job his impotence before God and pointing him to the importance of trusting Him.

God then described the fierce reptile's remarkable anatomy. Anyone gazing on a zoo-kept crocodile today can appreciate the words about the beasts' "limbs," "mighty strength," and "orderly frame" (41:12). His thick scales are like a soldier's metal armor, with double, impenetrable thickness (41:13). The crocodile's long jaws, poetically portrayed as "the doors of his face" cannot be pried open by hand, and his numerous teeth alongside his jaws

181

are terrifying (41:14). His scales are close together, thus adding to the difficulty of penetrating to his inner vitals (41:15-17).

The sneezes of the crocodile "flash forth light"; that is, "the spray forced through his nostrils appears to flash light in the bright sun."[45] But why are his eyes said to be "like the eyelids of the morning" (41:18)? The small eyes, with catlike slits for pupils, are the first part of the animal that a person sees when it emerges from the water. Thus its pupils gradually emerging above the surface of the water may be compared to the sun's rays gradually emerging above the horizon (see 3:9, marg., where Job likened the dawn's rays to a person's eyelids). Related to this verse is the observation that "in Egyptian hieroglyphs, the eye of the crocodile represents dawn."[46]

The fire from the mouth and the smoke from the nostrils (41:19-21) are often cited as evidence that the creature here is a mythical dragon. However, those fiery phenomena may also be explained as the poet's way of depicting the expelling of the crocodile's "pent-up breath together with water in a hot stream from its mouth [which] looks like a stream of fire in the sunshine."[47] The verses certainly should not be understood as giving credence to the belief that the Ugaritic Lotan actually existed.[48]

Because of the amphibian's strong neck, people run from him in dismay (41:22). His flesh is hard, unlike the flabby, leatherlike hide of the hippopotamus, and his heart is as hard as the bottom of two millstones (41:23-24). It is no wonder, then, that when this beast of the sea rises (out of the water), even the strongest of humans are afraid, and that they are bewildered (literally, beside themselves) when they see the breakers of the sea (41:25).

Hunters' weapons, including the sword,[49] spear, dart, javelin, arrow, slingstones, club, and saber,[50] are of no avail to fell the

45. Reichert, p. 216.
46. Ibid.
47. Rowley, p. 337.
48. See *The Zondervan Pictorial Encyclopedia of the Bible,* s.v. "Leviathan," by H. L. Ellison, 3:912.
49. "The sword that reaches him cannot avail" suggests that even if a person dares to get close enough to him to wield a sword, it will do no good (41:26).
50. Although the NASB translates the last weapon in 41:29 as "javelin," the Hebrew word differs from the word rendered "javelin" in 41:26. "Saber" seems to be closer to the meaning in 41:29.

crocodile. Weapons of iron and bronze break as easily as straw and wood (41:26-29). The hide of the crocodile's underside is jagged like the pointed edges of broken pottery; and when he walks across mud, the sharp scales on his underside leave marks like those left by a threshing sledge (41:30). Swimming in a river or sea, the crocodile churns up the water like a boiling pot and like "a jar of ointment," meaning the foam on the top of the ingredients of an ointment being boiled or stirred by an apothecary (41:31). "Behind him he makes a wake to shine" (41:32a) is literally "behind him he lights a path" and means that as he moves swiftly through the water he leaves behind what appears to be a path. His churning of the water makes whitecaps on the surface, giving it the appearance of white hair (41:32b).

The crocodile is incomparable, for God has created him to be fearless (41:33). Because he is supreme, he looks down on all other animals. He is king over all "the sons of pride," that is, over proud beasts (41:34; see 28:8).

4. *Job's second reply to God* (42:1-6)

Animals independent of man (38:39—39:30) and animals dangerous and repulsive to man (40:15—41:34) were all a grand zoological exhibition to help Job sense that because he had nothing to do with making, sustaining, or even subduing them, it was unthinkable that he could question their Creator. Anyone who cannot undertake God's works has no right to undermine God's ways. And anyone who trembles at the sight of fierce beasts is unwise in boldly contending with the beasts' Maker.

Having contemplated the overpowering strength and frightening fierceness of Behemoth and Leviathan, and his resultant incompetence to capture them easily, Job appreciated anew the unlimited depths of the wisdom, majesty, and omnipotence of God. Faced with divine splendor in the sky, on the earth, and under the earth, Job was led by this natural revelation to realize God's all-embracing power: "I know that Thou canst do all things" (42:2a); here Job's sense of awe and submission is implied. Because of God's power, His sovereign purposes will be carried out: "no purpose of Thine can be thwarted" (42:2b). Because

God's intentions cannot be altered or disrupted ("thwarted" means "cut off," literally), Job saw that it was useless for him to question God's actions.

Job then repeated God's initial question to him, "Who is this that hides counsel without knowledge?" (42:3a; cf. 38:2). The purpose of the repetition was to admit to the justice of the rebuke implied in it.[51] Job admitted that he was the one who had spoken presumptuously of wonderful things that were beyond his comprehension (42:3b-c).

Job again repeated (42:4) what God had said to him at the beginning of each of His speeches (38:3; 40:7): "I will ask you, and you instruct [or answer] Me." Job then answered God, but not with the bold argumentation that he had formerly planned. Instead, he said that he saw God and that he repented. His present awareness of God compared with his former knowledge was like seeing compared with hearing—a direct, personal (and thus more thorough) knowledge compared with information gained indirectly or secondhand through tradition. (This is not the fulfillment of 19:25-27, in which Job affirmed God's future stand on the earth in final vindication after his death.) His previous theology had had no room for the suffering of a godly person; such suffering would have then suggested that God was unjust, and that proposition was theologically untenable. Now, however, Job's views were changed. How? By God's natural-science display, which not only deepened Job's impressions of God's wisdom and power, but also dramatically displayed what Job had doubted: God's providential care. This seeing was spiritual insight, not a physical vision.

Having deeper insight into God's character—His power, purposes, and providence—Job gained a more accurate view of his own finitude: "Therefore I retract, and I repent in dust and ashes" (42:6).[52] By using the word "retract," which means "to despise or reject,"[53] Job was saying that he rejected (a) his accu-

---

51. Reichert, p. 219.
52. A similar response was experienced by Isaiah (Isa 6:1-7) and Peter (Luke 5:8).
53. "I abhor myself" (KJV) does not properly convey the thought. Job had said that he despised his miserable condition (9:21), and "I waste away" (7:16a) is literally "I despise" or "I reject" with no object of the verb expressed, as in 42:6.

sations and claims against God, his statements about "things too wonderful for [him], which [he] did not know" (42:3), or (b) his attitude of rebellious pride, or (c) both. Because the Hebrew does not state what he despised or rejected, it may be that both his accusations and his attitude were involved. One may well imply the other.

Elihu had warned him of the error of his charges against God (33:9-13; 34:31-33; 35:2-3; 36:23) and of the error of his attitude of pride (32:2; 33:17; 35:12-13; 36:9; 37:24). And God Himself had confronted Job with his proud audacity to indict Him (40:2) and to condemn Him (40:8).

Job's concluding words were: "I repent in dust and ashes" (42:6). Throwing dust in the air so that it came down on one's head (cf. 2:12) and sitting on ashes (cf. 2:8; Isa 58:5; Dan 9:3; Jonah 3:6) were signs of a humbled condition because of grief over sin or over a catastrophe. The disfiguring of one's external appearance was designed to express the turmoil of his inner soul. Job's repentance, then, was one of deep humility.[54]

But of what did Job repent? Obviously he did not repent of the charges his three consolers had brought against him. His oath of innocence (chap. 31) and God's assessment of him (1:1, 8; 2:3) prove the falsity of their accusations of sins committed before his calamities. Job repented of his proud rebellion, of his impudent insistence that God respond to him and that he correct His ways.[55] Job, then, admitted to sinning because he suffered, not to suffering because he sinned.

God's speeches did not reveal Him to be lacking in compassion. Instead, they showed that He is interested in communicating with man, that He desires to be known personally as well as intellectually. This personal, indescribable knowledge of the divine underscores the finiteness of man's character before God, the futility of man's complaints against God, and the satisfaction that comes from man's communion with God.

---

54. This was all the more remarkable in view of his already sitting on ashes. Having expressed grief over his losses, he now expressed grief over his sin.
55. The context (42:2-5) suggests that Job's repentance was more than a turning from his remorseful condition of sitting on the ash pile, as suggested recently by Dale Patrick ("The Translation of Job XLII 6," *Vetus Testamentum* 26 [July 1976]:369-71.

13

Living with Mystery

III. EPILOGUE (42:7-17)

The book closes in prose, as it had begun (chaps. 1—2). In the epilogue, attention is given to Job's friends (42:7-9) and then to Job's fortunes (42:10-17).

A. GOD AND JOB'S FRIENDS (42:7-9)

Job had asked the three counselors, "Will it be well when He examines you?" (13:9), and here the answer was no. God spoke to Eliphaz, as the representative of the three, and said that He was angry with them "because you [plural] have not spoken of Me what is right as My servant Job has" (42:7). But what had they said about God that was wrong? Had they not defended His justice and spoken of His power, and was not Job the one who had arraigned His justice? How could God lead Job to repentance and then say that he had spoken the truth? The answer lies in the fact that the three friends, in their effort to uphold God's justice, had limited His sovereignty. Their insistence that suffering must always be God's judgment on sin boxed God in; it said, "God can act only in this way." And that was not right! (Job himself had accused them of speaking "what is unjust for God" and "what is deceitful for Him" [13:7].)

On the other hand, Job "had consistently maintained that he had not by sin called down this punishment from God, and this was a right thing to say about God."[1] Furthermore, although Job questioned God's justice and despised God's silence, he did repent of it; and he had consistently elaborated on God's power, sovereignty, knowledge, and wisdom. In fact, his view of God was higher than the view of the three counselors.

1. H. H. Rowley, *Job,* p. 344.

186

God commanded the three counselors to offer a burnt offering of seven bulls and seven rams, a large sacrifice, which indicated the gravity of their error (42:8). Ironically, Job then prayed for those who had falsely accused him. Serving again as a priest (cf. 1:5), he was to aid in their sacrifice, praying that God would accept them. His readiness to intercede on their behalf demonstrated his willingness to forgive them and thus showed again the depth of his godly character. He had maligned God and was forgiven when he repented; now it was his turn to forgive those who had maligned him and were repenting. No wonder God called him "My servant" four times in these two verses! They did as God instructed them to do, and God accepted Job's intercessory prayer (42:9). Their expiatory sacrifice prevented them from receiving what they deserved because of their foolish words (42:8). Earlier, Zophar had said that God was not giving Job half of what he deserved by way of punishment (11:6). No doubt Zophar was now grateful that God had not given *him* what *he* deserved!

It is striking that with all their talk about Job's need to admit his sin and be forgiven by God, *they* were now the ones to repent and experience God's—and Job's—forgiveness. Interestingly, Elihu was not included, apparently because he had spoken accurately about God.

B. GOD AND JOB'S FORTUNES (42:10-17)

Job was honored by God's restoring him double all the possessions he had lost (42:10, 12). And the restoration was after he had prayed for his friends, not after he had repented. Now that he was restored to his house (and presumably to his health and respected position in the community), his brothers, sisters, and acquaintances (who had forsaken him [19:13-14]) visited him, ate with him, comforted him,[2] and brought him gifts of silver, money,[3] and a gold ring (the last of those acts being a token of kindness to a person restored from calamity). In addi-

---

2. The "evil" that "the LORD had brought on him" was calamity, not moral evil.
3. The word translated "piece of money" meant uncoined silver, a word used elsewhere only in Genesis 33:19 and Joshua 24:32 regarding Jacob, an indication of a patriarchal date for the events in Job.

tion to restoring his livestock to amounts double what he had had before (42:12; cf. 1:3), which presumably took time, God gave Job ten more children, again seven sons and three daughters (42:13). The emptiness from the loss of his first offspring, however, could never be filled by the addition of others. Three interesting facts are included about the daughters: (1) their names were revealed, whereas the sons remain to us anonymous (42:14), (2) they were unusually beautiful, and (3) they, along with their brothers, were designated as heirs of Job's estate (42:15). Why the three daughters were named is unknown; perhaps it was to draw attention to their unusual role in bringing blessing to Job in his posttrial days. "Jemima" means "dove," "Keziah" means "perfume" (cassia being a bark used as a perfume), and "Keren-happuch" means "horn of eyepaint" (i.e., a bottle of dye used to paint the eyelashes, eyelids, and eyebrows to make the eyes more attractive). All three names were indicative of the daughters' beauty. Their share in their father's inheritance may have been his expression of gratitude for his new family or proof of his restored wealth.[4]

After his calamities, Job lived an additional 140 years, thus making a total of around 200. His ten children prior to his losses had been grown, so Job was supposedly about 60 or 70 years of age. If tradition is correct that he lived to be 210, Job's latter years were double his former years (140 compared with 70). That reckoning is possible though uncertain. Job "saw his sons, and his grandsons, four generations" (42:16) could mean that Job saw his posterity to the fourth generation. The patriarch, "an old man," died "full of days," having reached an honored old age.

Some readers have reasoned that his restored wealth and family proved after all the three counselors' theory that upright actions are rewarded. However, the restored fortunes were tokens of God's grace. God was freely bestowing His goodness, not obligingly rewarding Job's piety. Also, the continuation of his trials would have undone the significance of Job's repentance, and would have indicated God's caprice and arbitrary malice. The suffering proved Satan's accusation against Job to be wrong, so

4. Francis I. Andersen, *Job: An Introduction and Commentary*, p. 294.

the suffering did not need to continue. "Any judge who left a defendant to languish in prison after he had been declared innocent would be condemned as iniquitous."[5] Furthermore, the book of Job does not deny the general rule, found repeatedly in the Scriptures, that God blesses the righteous. Instead, it says that the principle is not invariable, that God by His sovereignty can withhold—or bestow—His blessings as He chooses for purposes known only to Him.

* * *

The book of Job, probably the oldest book in the Bible, deals profoundly—and surprisingly—with the world's most pressing and fundamental problems: the place of suffering and man's relationship to God. The book began with Satan's charge that Job was serving God for the profit motive, that his piety was payment for blessing. God took up the challenge because Satan's insinuations belittled both man and God. If Satan had been correct—if the motive of God's servant was selfish and if God must bribe man to worship Him—the very foundations of a true love relationship between God and man are destroyed. If God must dangle rewards in front of man to entice him to spirituality, God becomes capricious. If man's goodness stems from a contract designed to ward off trouble, piety becomes hypocrisy. Satan's charge, then, was profoundly serious. Such a devastating accusation could not go unanswered. The reputations of both God and man were at stake.

Yet Job knew nothing of this heavenly wager.[6] Without his even knowing it, Job had the honor of being used by God to refute the slanderer, to silence Satan. Job's refusal to curse God for withholding some of His blessings communicated to the world that the archenemy was wrong, that worship can be genuine, that man can serve God "for nothing" (1:9).

This is one of the grand purposes in the book, to deal with motive behind worship, to demonstrate that it is possible to view life as other than a give-and-get bargain with God. Job illustrates that although a man in his suffering may question God, he need

5. Rowley, p. 343.
6. However, if Job later wrote the book, he would have known by divine revelation the origin of his problem.

not curse God when he gets less than what he thinks he deserves. God is not a cosmic Santa Claus giving gifts only to good children and withholding them from the bad.

Job's sufferings, in addition to being a demonstration to Satan that pure worship is possible, served another purpose: to deepen his spiritual insights into the character of God.[7] Surely this contest was more than a wager between Satan and God, with Job being a helpless pawn on a cosmic chessboard. Whereas Satan intended to use this event to move Job away from God, God's intentions were that the afflictions open the way for Job to experience a greater comprehension of His person and His grace.[8]

Another central truth captioned across the pages of the book is that man can trust God even when explanations are missing. Man must live with mystery. He must recognize that his questions may remain unanswered, that God may choose to respond in silence to his inquiries about the reason for undeserved suffering, that God may remain silent to his probings about the problem of unmerited tragedy. The Christian must learn to remain content with problems he cannot understand, realizing that man's finitude keeps him from having eternity's perspective, which only God possesses. Like Job, we can learn that God's silence does not mean His absence.

It is for this reason that the book of Job teaches us another solemn lesson: the futility of criticizing God's ways. God's all-powerful sovereignty accentuates the folly of mere man's insisting that God report to him or run His universe according to his orders. The vast difference between God and man revealed to Job that he could not fully explain God. The cosmic chasm between the infinite and the finite enabled him to live with suffering, and to relinquish any claims against the Sovereign.

Job learned that effrontery in accusing God of injustice was sin—and we too should learn the error of challenging God's will and wisdom. A high view of the greatness of God should deepen

7. Eliphaz, Bildad, and Zophar insisted that the purpose in the suffering was *discipline* (punishment for wrongdoing); Job felt its purpose was *destruction* ("God is out to destroy me"); Elihu underscored the aim of affliction as *direction* (to keep man from the pit); and God had two objectives: *demonstration* (that Satan's accusation was false) and *development* (of Job's spiritual comprehension).
8. William Henry Green, *The Argument of the Book of Job Unfolded*, p. 291.

our sense of humility and awe before Him, removing from us pride and self-sufficiency.

But there is a positive side too. Not only must we live with problems unsolved and mysteries unfathomed. And not only must we willfully avoid presumptuous accusations against God. We must also trust Him, being aware of His presence and benevolence. Although Job did not obtain the solutions to his intellectual problems, he was reassured by the Problem-Solver. By having met God Himself, Job's soul was filled and overwhelmed with a deepened sense of His majesty.

By coming to know God more intimately (42:5), the patriarch "now confides in him more thoroughly than before. . . . [Job] now believes that the Most High cannot do any thing that is out of harmony with His perfections. All that He does must be right and glorious."[9] Job was not able to fathom God's mysteries, yet he came to trust the all-perfect God more fully, to realize that God is equally as loving when He sends afflictions as when He sends prosperity.[10]

Job and his consolers came to see that God, to be God, must be totally free. If God is predictable or is responsible to man, He ceases to be God. We too, in an attitude of calm trust, must allow God the freedom to be Himself.

Having been made more aware that God is *God,* Job asked no more questions. He then knew that he could live with his problems, unanswered as they were, because he knew that God had not forsaken him. Like Job, we can contemplate the rain and the raven, the dawn and the donkey, the stupid ostrich and the fierce crocodile, and realize that God's care for them implies His care for us. His creation and control of nature assure us of His all-sufficient ability to care for us too. Instead of searching frantically for an elusive answer to the perennial "why?" the Christian can enjoy life by resting in God. Instead of pounding the walls in angered frustration, he can quietly accept God's designs, knowing that His grace is sufficient (2 Cor 12:9), that His way is perfect (Psalm 18:30, marg.), and that, as Job learned, He is "full of compassion and is merciful" (James 5:11).

9. Ibid., p. 311.
10. Ibid.

Selected Bibliography

Andersen, Francis I. *Job: An Introduction and Commentary*. Downers Grove, Ill.: InterVarsity, 1976.

Baker, Wesley C. *More Than a Man Can Take: A Study of Job*. Philadelphia: Westminster, 1966.

Barnes, Albert. *Notes, Critical, Illustrative, and Practical, on the Book of Job*. 2 vols. Glasgow: Blackie & Son, 1847.

Davidson, A. B. *The Book of Job*. Cambridge: Cambridge U., 1903.

Dhorme, E. *A Commentary on the Book of Job*. Translated by Harold Knight. New York: Nelson, 1967.

Driver, Samuel Rolles, and Gray, George Buchanan. *A Critical and Exegetical Commentary on the Book of Job*. The International Critical Commentary. Edinburgh: T. & T. Clark, 1921.

Ellison, H. L. *A Study of Job: From Tragedy to Triumph*. Grand Rapids: Zondervan, 1971.

Gordis, Robert. *The Book of God and Man: A Study of Job*. Chicago: U. of Chicago, 1965.

Green, William Henry. *The Argument of the Book of Job Unfolded*. 1874. Reprint, Minneapolis: James and Klock, 1977.

Howard, David. *How Come, God?* Philadelphia: Holman, 1972.

Johnson, L. D. *Israel's Wisdom: Learn and Live*. Nashville: Broadman, 1975.

————. *Out of the Whirlwind: The Major Message of the Book of Job*. Nashville: Broadman, 1971.

Kent, H. Harold. *Job Our Contemporary*. Grand Rapids: Eerdmans, 1967.

Pope, Marvin H. *Job*. 3d ed. The Anchor Bible. Garden City, N.Y.: Doubleday, 1973.

Reichert, Victor E. *Job*. London: Soncino, 1946.

Rowley, H. H. *Job*. The Century Bible. Greenwood, S.C.: Attic, 1970.

Schaper, Robert N. *Why Me, God?* Glendale, Calif.: Regal, 1974.